UNDER THE WIG

UNDER THE WIG

A Lawyer's Stories of Murder, Guilt and Innocence

William Clegg QC

Canbury Press

First published by Canbury Press 2018

This edition published 2018

Canbury Press

Kingston upon Thames, Surrey

www.canburypress.com

Cover: Moker Ontwerp, Netherlands

Printed and bound in Great Britain by Clays Ltd, Elcograf S.p.A.

This is a work of non-fiction.

The events and experiences detailed herein are true and have been faithfully rendered to the best of the author's ability.

ISBN: 978-1-912454-08-2 Hardback

978-1-912454-09-9 Ebook

978-1-912454-11-2 Audiobook

For my wife Gay
and
my children and step-children
Joanna, Peter, Robert & Candice

CONTENTS

INTRODUCTION

How can you defend a man like that?

~

How can I defend someone who I know is guilty? It's the question I am asked the most often. It is really a velvet glove on some finger-pointing: how can I, a decent man, speak up for a rapist or murderer? How can I put my professional skills and intellect at the disposal of someone who has committed such a terrible crime?

All advocates are asked this question, perhaps me more than most because of the nature of my career. I have defended more than 100 people accused of murder, probably more than any other lawyer practising in England. The first thing to say is that in English law to defend somebody who I know in the strict sense of the word is guilty is not allowed. If the client tells me they are guilty, I must not tell a court they are innocent.

For crimes such as fraud or drugs, a client may freely acknowledge what they have done and plead guilty, perhaps after I have pointed out the strength of the case against them and told them of the reduced sentence that greets a guilty plea. This happens often; I don't varnish the facts.

Murder, though, is different. Murder is killing someone with the intention of causing them serious harm or death and a sentence of life imprisonment automatically follows for anyone who pleads guilty or is convicted by a jury. The most that is given is a minor reduction in the tariff, the minimum jail time that must be served before parole is considered, which is little incentive to admit guilt.

So a client will not usually tell me they have committed murder. They may, however, tell me that they did the killing, but in circumstances that would generate a partial or complete defence. For instance, they may say they were acting in self-defence — which is a complete defence to murder and will absolve guilt for a killing.

Or they may rely on one of several defences unique to murder, which will reduce the offence to manslaughter, making the sentence at the discretion of the judge. So my client may admit they did the act, but claim that they were provoked, which is a partial defence. Or they may say there were suffering from an abnormality of the mind such that they had diminished responsibility, which also reduces the offence to manslaughter. So I have to weigh up all the evidence to see which defences may be open.

I like to meet a client as soon as possible after they have been arrested. In a murder case, they are unlikely to be released on bail, to resume their ordinary life while awaiting a trial. Instead they are usually held in a prison. When visiting them, the guards will check I am not taking in contraband such as drugs or any metal objects that could be made into a weapon. My papers and bags will be X-rayed and my watch, wallet, phone and keys will be put in a locker. I am allowed to take in the case papers, minus any metal clasps that hold them together, and normally one pen. The prisoner will usually only have loose papers — they are not usually permitted any files.

We will meet in a small room with glass panels, so that the prison officers can look in but not listen. A small Formica table and chairs will be screwed to the floor so the prisoner can't pick them up and use them as a weapon.

This first meeting is normally tense. When you meet a murder defendant for the first time they are facing just about the most important event in their life: a trial that may confine them to prison for the rest of their days; and I, a stranger, am coming to discuss it. Prisoners share information and each will have his favourite barristers; there will be no shortage of inmates advising your client whether you are good, bad or indifferent.

By the time of the first meeting, I will already have an idea of the prisoner's circumstances. Their solicitor will have assembled and typed up for me a Proof of Evidence, which is an account of what they are saying. (A solicitor is a lawyer who takes the instructions of the accused and prepares their case, but does not usually represent them in court. As the barrister, I represent the client in court.)

On a first meeting, though, I may not talk about the case in any detail at all. I will probably mention it in rather general terms and focus on trying to build up a rapport. The key thing is to put the client at ease. I may talk about the weather, I may talk about where they live, what work they do. I will ask them how they are getting on in prison, what sort of visits they are having; has the family been able to visit them? One client desperately missed his dog, so we chatted about that. The most important thing is to gain the accused's trust; unless I can establish trust between them and myself, I am never going to represent them successfully.

This is not always easy. Much may depend on the client's character. Some may have a limited education or may have mental health problems, or may not have English as their first language. Worst of all is talking through an interpreter, which makes life very difficult.

Other defendants may have excellent university degrees, probably better than mine. Many, though, come from fairly ordinary backgrounds. They often perceive that I am from a different class, which is not surprising. By the time the average barrister gets to represent a murder defendant, they are probably well into middle age. They wear a suit and have a 'posh' accent. They seem to be part of the establishment. I try to break down these barriers, but I can only do so much. I can't pretend to be the same as a teenage gang member; that would be ludicrous. I am a 69-year-old lawyer. I will remain part of the establishment. The best I can often hope for is that the client thinks I am on their side.

By the time I see them they have normally got over the shock of being arrested and charged and being in prison. Clients rarely get very emotional or hysterical before the start of their trial. There are alarms that I can press to summon assistance, but in my five decades as a barrister, I have never been threatened or assaulted by a defendant. I am there to help them.

Most murderers have never been in trouble with the law before: the person most likely to murder you is your parent or your partner or your child. The murder weapon is seldom a sawn-off shotgun. It's more likely to be a pillow over a child's face. I have felt genuine sympathy with some people charged with murder in the home. One can see how a mother living without a partner has been pushed to the limit by very difficult circumstances without any help or support.

As to morality, it's not for me to judge whether someone is guilty or innocent: that's why we have a trial. But in a way the question as to how a barrister can defend a murderer — or alleged murderer — is more important than that, because any effective system of criminal justice must have a mechanism for people accused of a crime to be defended. If people aren't defended, we won't have justice.

For this reason, with a few exceptions, I cannot pick and choose which client I represent. A barrister must wait for the next client to arrive, whoever it is. The 'cab rank' principle is there to ensure that everybody has access to justice. After all, if a lawyer could pick and choose cases they might only choose winnable ones; unpopular clients such as terrorists would be left without a lawyer because no-one would represent them. The only reason I can turn a case down is if I am already committed elsewhere, if I already represent another party in the same case, if there is a conflict of interest, or if the fee is below my normal charge. That said, for a very special case, about an interesting or important point of law, I might see if I can juggle court dates to accommodate it.

What I do not do is reject a case because I suspect I will dislike the client, or think he is guilty. I have certainly done some cases where the defendants have been so vilified by the press that they have become a hate figure. Some have turned out to be entirely innocent. Had they not been properly represented, they may well have been the victim of a miscarriage of justice and been locked up for decades.

On the other hand, sometimes the prosecution evidence is overwhelming. Of course it's only after I have accepted a case from a solicitor that I realise it is hopeless — nobody will pay me to read the papers until I have taken it on. I can't rely too much on the synopsis drafted by my solicitor because they are inclined to make a brief sound enormously attractive. In such cases, where the evidence is convincing, I advise the defendant that unless they can provide a credible explanation for the following aspect of the evidence — like their fingerprints on the gun, their DNA on the corpse or CCTV showing them opening fire — then a verdict of not guilty is going to be extremely unlikely and they would perhaps like to reflect on that and plead guilty.

A client is naturally curious about what jail term they might get. If they wish me to defend them at trial, they must not tell me that they have committed the crime alleged. But they might say: 'Hypothetically, were I to plead guilty, what do you think the sentence would be?' I would be able to advise those facing charges other than murder that by pleading guilty at this stage their sentence would be X years. But, hypothetically, if they were to plead not guilty and be found guilty at a trial their sentence would be 25 per cent longer. Then a defendant can weigh up the benefit of pleading guilty against the likelihood of a not guilty verdict at trial.

If they say 'No, I'm not guilty, I didn't do it', then I must proceed with the case. I have fought many absurd and hopeless cases. I can't avoid a trial by refusing to defend someone who declines to put in what others would consider to be a sensible and timely plea of guilty. In these cases, I don't just go through the motions: I present the case as best I can. If I have advised a client that the evidence against them is overwhelming, I have restful nights. I can rely on the jury to come to a sensible conclusion on the evidence.

It's much more difficult to defend someone whom I suspect is not guilty. I try not to think 'They have definitely got the wrong person and this man is innocent' because that creates a very real pressure. The thought that an innocent man may be incarcerated for the rest of their life because I have failed to expose the weaknesses in the case against him means I don't sleep at all well at night. It is a worry that gnaws. This was the case with the man who was missing his dog.

CHAPTER ONE

Case 1
The Wimbledon Common Murder

~

Some crimes are so savage and so unsettling that detectives come under an almost unbearable pressure to solve them. In this case, Rachel Nickell, a 23-year-old mother, found herself in the wrong place at the wrong time when she went for a walk on Wimbledon Common, south-west London, on 15 July 1992.

Rachel was with her three-year-old son, Alex, and their labrador, Molly, when a man dragged her into the undergrowth, sexually assaulted her, stabbed her 49 times, and cut her throat. Alex was found by a passer-by clinging to his mother's blood-soaked body, desperately pleading with her to wake up.

Rachel was especially photogenic and the fact that her

young son had witnessed the murder, and that it had happened in daylight in much-loved heathland in the capital thrust the murder to the top of the news headlines, where it remained for weeks.

The pressure on London's police force to catch Ms Nickell's killer was intense. Unfortunately for the Metropolitan Police no-one saw the bloodied killer leaving the common. No forensic evidence from the crime-scene identified a suspect. Under the relentless gaze of the media, the investigators turned to a new development in police inquiries: criminal profiling. A psychologist, Paul Britton, was asked to create a psychological assessment of the kind of individual who would have committed the crime.

Britton gave the police a description of the man they should be seeking. He would be a sexually repressed loner who lived on his own close to the scene of the crime. He would be in his twenties or thirties. He would have an interest in the occult and in knives and be sexually repressed.

The police made door-to-door inquiries in the area around Wimbledon Common and questioned more than 30 men. They also broadcast a photofit picture of two unidentified men seen on the common, one with long hair, another with short hair. Four callers identified the short-haired man as Colin Stagg, a 31-year-old unemployed man who lived locally.

Just as Britton had predicted, Colin was something of a loner. Like Ms Nickell, he enjoyed walking his dog,

Brandy, on the common. He had no previous convictions, but during the three days he was questioned by police he admitted that he had sunbathed naked in a secluded patch of the common and that a woman may have seen him doing so.

A woman whom Colin had been in touch with after she responded to a lonely hearts advert also contacted detectives: Colin, she said, had written to her graphically suggesting various sexual activity they could engage in. Detectives also found some books on the occult in Colin's flat. A witness described seeing a man fitting Colin's appearance on the common at around the time the murder took place and subsequently picked him out at an identity parade.

In the police's eyes, Colin had become the prime suspect. The pieces of the jigsaw were falling into place. The only problem was the lack of hard evidence. It was true that Colin had been on the common that day and one witness had picked him out at an identity parade. But that was it — not a speck of forensic evidence linked him to the crime scene. Police were forced to release their prime suspect without charge.

They then asked Britton to design a covert operation to prove or disprove that an unidentified suspect killed Ms Nickell. Britton suggested that if a woman were to befriend the suspect and feign interest in violent sexual fantasies he might end up admitting to her that he was the murderer. Operation Ezdell was duly launched. An attractive female undercover officer was asked to pose as the friend of a woman Colin had previously contacted through the lonely hearts column. 'Lizzie James' (a pseudonym) embarked on five months of phone calls, letters and four meetings with Colin, all of which were recorded for use as evidence. Throughout she feigned a sexual interest in Colin and they traded sexual fantasies. She held out the lure of sex as bait.

Colin was a virgin and he admitted to Lizzie that he had occasional fantasies involving violence, but at no point did he admit any involvement in Ms Nickell's murder, despite Lizzie repeatedly raising it in conversation. At one point she dangled her sexual compliance to him in exchange for him confessing all, telling Colin: 'If only you had done the Wimbledon Common murder. If only you had killed her, it would be alright.' Colin replied: 'I'm terribly sorry, but I haven't.' That should have been enough to end the honey trap. But instead Mr Britton changed tack saying instead that the conversations between Colin and Lizzie James, although not including any admission to the killing, were sufficient to satisfy him that Colin must be the killer.

A short time later Colin was re-arrested and charged with Rachel's murder. He spent almost a year on remand in Brixton Prison awaiting trial. From the moment I met Colin in prison, he struck me as a most improbable murderer. There appeared to be no conceivable motive for someone who had never been in trouble before committing such an appalling and uncharacteristic crime. He didn't seem to be remotely aggressive and in fact came across as a rather passive individual. I thought it said a lot about him that many of his neighbours signed a card wishing him luck, which I do not remember happening in any other murder trial.

I saw Colin seven or eight times in prison in the run-up to the trial, which started in September 1994, to take instructions and to build up a rapport. He wasn't unintelligent. He was rather immature, but was living a perfectly contented life in a small council flat. We had pretty much nothing in common apart from the fact that we both had dogs called Brandy. He adored his dog. It was put into kennels at a dogs' home after he was remanded to Brixton. At one point Colin became convinced that Brandy had died and the thought preoccupied him to the exclusion of everything else. He once went on hunger strike for several days over something to do with his dog. My junior Jim Sturman went down to the kennels to visit it on one occasion. Sometimes when I saw Colin he was more worried about the dog than he was about himself.

Colin's case was due to be tried like all serious cases in Britain before a jury of 12 members of the public, who would decide whether he was guilty after listening to the evidence presented by both sides.

It was scheduled to be heard at the Central Criminal Court, better known as the Old Bailey — the biggest and most historic criminal court in London. Heading up the prosecution were a leading barrister, a junior barrister and some solicitors. Our defence team comprised a leading barrister (me), a junior barrister (Jim Sturman) and a solicitor. As well as defending Colin, we were there to support him. He didn't have any friends or family at court. He had started a relationship with a woman while he was in custody, but she hadn't met him in person by that stage and she wasn't in court.

Before the jury start their work, the defence and prosecution can argue over procedural aspects of the case. This legal argument takes place in open court, but the media can't report what is said until after the case, so that jurors don't hear any evidence that the judge rules is inadmissible.

Before the jury was sworn in at the Old Bailey I sought to exclude Lizzie James's evidence. The legal argument lasted three days, during which I contended that it was preposterous to view Colin's denial to her of any involvement in Ms Nickell's killing as a tacit admission on his part that he had killed her. I also disputed the expertise of Mr Britton, the psychologist, arguing that his opinion was not properly to be admitted as expert evidence. When one analysed what he had done, I argued, he was relying on guesswork and supposition.

I argued that Colin was being tricked by the police into saying things that the criminal profiler claimed were incriminating, and that it was about as far from a case of him volunteering information to an undercover police officer (which would have been perfectly admissible) as one could conceive. This was the reverse — the police were manipulating Colin and controlling the conversations in an attempt to direct him as to what he would say.

My opposite number, John Nutting, did his best to counteract the force of my submission. He had accepted the case at short notice after another barrister had dropped out. It was obvious to John, I'm sure, that it was a very difficult case to present because of the way detectives had gathered the evidence.

At the end of the legal argument, the judge, Mr Justice Ognall retired for almost a week to consider what both sides had said. Notwithstanding the importance of the decision, that was quite a long time. In a high-profile case like that a judge is very anxious to arrive at the correct ruling. Apart from anything else if they get it wrong, it will be overturned at the Court of Appeal, which is embarrassing.

We were confident about our argument, but we were not sure we would win. Nowadays you might get a draft copy of a judgment before you go into court, but that wasn't so here. Mr Justice Ognall started by reviewing all the evidence before reading out his ruling for more than an hour. The courtroom was tense as everyone sat in silence waiting to find out what would happen. But as I listened, I started to get an inkling. Then there came a moment when I knew we had won: the judge was going to exclude Lizzie James's evidence. Once it was knocked out the prosecution had no evidence to offer and Colin was formally found not guilty. He sat in the dock behind us, looking shellshocked. We locked eyes and I smiled, but he didn't really react.

After half an hour Colin was finally released from the cells below the court and gave me a hug. It was quite emotional. I had warmed to him by that stage. I sometimes get very close to my clients when I am contributing to what will probably be the most important moment in their lives. I feel I could sensibly become friends with some of them. Colin did not fall into that category, but I was genuinely delighted he had been found not guilty because I knew it was the right verdict.

There was a huge media scrum outside the Old Bailey but we managed to spirit Colin away out the back door and he was driven off to my chambers in a taxi. Unfortunately, immediately after the case collapsed the police gave a press conference at which they said they weren't looking for anybody else for Ms Nickell's murder – the classic thing they say when they want to imply that a judge has let a guilty man off. Colin had been pilloried in the press since he was first arrested and the police were giving off-the-record briefings to journalists to the effect that he had escaped justice because of a technicality.

If the evidence collected by the undercover police officer had been allowed into the trial, I don't think it would have swayed the jury, but you can never be sure. Juries do unpredictable things. I think the police officers had convinced themselves that Colin had murdered Ms

Nickell. They became so desperate to solve the murder that they thought it must be him because they couldn't imagine it being anyone else.

At any rate, Colin had been found not guilty. The ruling was probably my single biggest victory up to that point and boosted my career. It created a bit of a precedent and has been relied upon in other cases since.

Had the trial gone ahead I would have enjoyed cross-examining Mr Britton. It could have been one of the great cross-examinations of my career, but I much preferred to win the case beforehand. Defence barristers will happily take the folding of the prosecution case above being able to tear into a witness. Had the undercover policewoman been called to give evidence I could not have been too hard on her. She would have simply said: 'I only did what the criminal profiler told me to do.' Her evidence would have been largely uncontroversial.

In my opinion the vast majority of work criminal profilers do is rubbish. I don't think there has been a single case where they have done the remotest good; what they do is based on guesswork. (I did an appeal many years ago where a criminal profiler, supposedly one of the finest in his field, prepared a report for the appeal stating that in his view a particular defendant was not guilty of murder and that his wife had committed suicide. Fair enough, perhaps — except that he had prepared a report saying the opposite, that the wife hadn't committed suicide, at the man's trial, saying on appeal that his original opinion was wrong!)

So far as Colin was concerned all that mattered was that he was reunited with Brandy, who fortunately recognised him even though they had been apart for months. I helped Colin negotiate the finer points of a deal with the *News of the World*. The paper offered him £100,000 for his story after he was cleared, but would only go ahead on condition that he took a lie detector test. I was very suspicious of this. I didn't have much faith in the tests and I had even less faith in the *News of the World*. I thought it was all a stitch-up, but that turned out not to be the case. He passed the lie detector test with flying colours and they paid him the money. I remember advising him that he should use it to buy his council flat. With a client like Colin, I can find myself giving personal as well as professional advice. I'm pretty sure Colin didn't buy his flat but I haven't seen him for many years.

Even after the trial collapsed nobody could be absolutely certain at that stage that Colin hadn't killed Rachel Nickell. But it was not long before I was convinced that I knew the identity of the man who had.

CHAPTER TWO

Perry Mason and the Art of Advocacy

~

Perry Mason made me want to become a barrister. He won American murder cases weekly on the black and white television in the sitting room of our family home in early 1960s England. I loved the drama of his plots and the theatre of his showdowns. Mason took on unpromising, almost hopeless cases; yet he never lost them and at the end of every episode the back door of the courtroom would break open and the crucial witness would walk through. As an advocate, Mason wasn't particularly flamboyant. He was very dignified and understated in an almost British way.

I became fixed on the idea of becoming a barrister, which I think my parents thought was a little over-ambitious. They ran a florist's shop in Westcliff-on-Sea, Essex, and there were no 'professionals' on either side of my family; my relatives were mostly shopkeepers or factory workers. I remember my father saying to me: 'If you want a good profession how about pharmacy? You could open a chemist's shop. If you did well you could open another one and start a chain of chemist's shops.' I think he could identify with a career like that more easily. He knew people who had chemist's shops and they did very well.

It looked like my parents' caution was well founded when I failed the Eleven Plus exams required for grammar school. Instead, I went to a Roman Catholic secondary modern school, St Thomas More, and then Westcliff High School for Boys, where I took A-Levels in history, geography and economics. My two As and a B won me a place at Bristol University to study for a Bachelor of Laws. (Oxford or Cambridge were out of the question: to study law there in those days you had to have O-Level Latin. Unsurprisingly, St Thomas More didn't include Latin in its curriculum.)

A full grant from Southend Council paid for my tuition fees and halls of residence, meaning I had breakfast, dinner and somewhere to sleep, and some change left over. I pitched myself into university life and had quite a hectic social life; I drank a lot of beer. But I wasn't a member of any outrageous dining clubs – I didn't have the money. An expensive night out was a pizza and a bottle of red wine.

In 1968, my first year at Bristol, students had rioted in

Paris and there was much publicity about student revolts and sit-ins at universities in England. I was only involved on the fringe, but I took part in anti-Apartheid demonstrations outside Barclays Bank and Gloucestershire Cricket Club, which had taken on the South African all-rounder Mike Procter. (I later realised how much he had done for the underprivileged in his country). I also took part in sit-ins. In truth they usually took place after we'd been out drinking; it was something to do to keep warm before you staggered home. My politics were broadly left-wing but the vast majority of my fellow students (who were to the left of Stalin) viewed me as a reactionary.

Of the 100 law students at Bristol in my year, most came from public schools and I was conscious I had a different background, not that anybody was condescending. My friends were mostly student engineers, architects and the like from the halls of residence, who came from a wider range of backgrounds. I don't think it did me any harm at all not mixing with my fellow lawyers. Going to a state school has helped me deal with clients throughout my career. But the privately-educated law students were brimming with confidence, which didn't come so naturally to me. I'm not remotely conscious of it now, but I was then.

We didn't actually do much law at university. We had about eight hours of lectures and a couple of tutorials per week and I didn't make them all, especially those in the mornings. I could probably have learned the law that was actually useful to me in three months.

My tutor was a barrister called George Forrest. As well as holding down a full-time lecturing post, Forrest had his own criminal practice. At 9am he would lecture to us and by 10.30am he would be at Shire Hall, the Assize Court in Bristol, defending someone on a murder charge. He was a very old-fashioned patrician lecturer, about 30 years older than the students. The eight of us who were in his tutorial group were occasionally invited to his house for sherry.

There were two advantages to having Forrest as my tutor. The first was that he sometimes gave us examples from his real cases to help with our studies. The second was that he introduced me to my Inn of Court, which is one of the essential staging posts in the life of a young barrister.

To practise as a barrister in England and Wales one must become a member of one of the four great Inns of Court (Lincoln's Inn, Inner Temple, Middle Temple and Gray's Inn), which have acted as the headquarters of the legal profession since the middle ages.

Forrest was a member of Gray's Inn and he kindly acted as my sponsor there while I was still at university. Although an honour, being introduced to Gray's Inn did not itself make me a barrister. I would need to pass my law degree, then enroll at the Inns of Court School of Law and pass further exams called the Bar Finals. But it would help me deal with one of the quirks of the English legal system arising from the hospitable history of the Inns of

Court. In those days you had to eat either 24 or 36 dinners before you could become a barrister. It was advisable to start eating before you had left university because unless you did so you might, quite literally, be left with too much on your plate. It was not just a question of eating the requisite number of dinners, you had to 'keep term' which involved eating three dinners in one of the four legal terms of the year. So, eating 36 dinners took three years. You could 'double dine' in a desperate bid to fit all your meals in and eat some dinners after being 'called' as a barrister, but there was a danger that the only reason you couldn't formally become a barrister was because you hadn't eaten enough meals.

All this meant that in my final year at Bristol I would drive to London and back in an evening in my yellow Mini just to dine at Gray's Inn. The food was very much like school dinners, accompanied by considerable quantities of sherry, wine and port. Senior lawyers and judges, called benchers, enjoyed a superior menu and wine on the top table, above those in the body of the hall.

Inevitably the end of my third year at Bristol came around too quickly and I had to sit my finals. I've always had a good memory and I swotted a lot, but I only scraped through my law exams. Perhaps my parents were right after all. By then, it didn't matter much. I had a law degree and had started eating my way towards becoming a barrister. After a summer of selling bread and cakes from a mobile van for the Co-op back in Westcliff-on-Sea, I had to take the Bar Exams, which required a further year of study at the Council of Legal Education. Again, my local authority provided me with a full grant and I moved into a house with other law students at a rent of £6 per week. Lectures usually took place from 9am until 6pm, but there were often evening sessions because some lecturers appeared in the courts during the day. Again, the course wasn't particularly relevant.

After passing my Bar Finals in June 1972, I achieved my ambition when I was watching Perry Mason a decade earlier: I was 'called to the Bar.'[1] In line with tradition I wore white tie and tails to the 'call ceremony', at the end of which the Treasurer of Honourable Society of Gray's Inn informed me: 'I do hereby call you to the Bar and do publish you barrister.' I was given a certificate which rather curiously confirmed that I had been published 'utter barrister'. Why the word 'utter' is used is unclear.

Like all the other new barristers I was given a slim book called *Duty and Art in Advocacy* written by the Honourable Sir Malcolm Hilbery and first published in 1946. Its 44 pages set out the ethics of the profession and its strictures remain true by and large today. My copy, which I still have, refers to the minimum fee for a barrister being increased from one to two guineas, although you were permitted, and indeed were expected, to give your services

---

1 This historic and quaint-sounding terms refers to a physical barrier in court that separated a barrister from the judges. To speak in court, you had to be 'called to the bar'.

free of charge on occasion to people who were unable to afford them. Guineas (one guinea was one pound and one shilling in old money) were no longer in circulation after decimalisation in 1971, but were still the preferred denomination of barristers.

Until being called to the bar I hadn't been able to wear my own wig and gown. Now I could put on the horsehair wig and gown that my parents had bought me from Thresher & Glenny in Chancery Lane by the Royal Courts of Justice. They came up from Southend one afternoon after court to witness the moment. It was proud day for me and for my parents.

CHAPTER THREE

Case 2
The Murder of Samantha Bisset

~

Even though 23 years have elapsed, I still vividly remember reading the legal papers provided to me by a firm of solicitors acting for a man accused of the murder of a young mother and her daughter in their home.

Samantha Bisset had opened the door of her one-bedroom flat in Plumstead, south London, to a strange man who stabbed her in the neck and forced his way into her home. She put up a desperate struggle, but was killed. The man mutilated her body with a seven-inch knife, slicing open her chest and leaving 60 stab wounds. Jazmine, who was four, was sexually assaulted and suffocated in her bed. Part of her mother's abdomen was cut out and taken away, apparently as a trophy.

In May 1994, a local man called Robert Napper was arrested on suspicion of the murders after a fingerprint of his was discovered inside Ms Bisset's basement flat. As I read further into the papers a chill crept up my spine. What disturbed me was not the grisly details of the killing, but the growing realisation that whoever had carried out the murders was almost certainly the same person who had killed Rachel Nickell on Wimbledon Common the year before.

As I read into the papers my mind reeled. There were a number of obvious similarities between the murders.

For a start, it is statistically very unusual for a stranger to murder a mother in the presence of a young child. Secondly, both killings took place either on or alongside common land – Ms Bisset's flat looked on to Winn's Common, while Ms Nickell's murder was on Wimbledon Common. Thirdly, both were stabbed numerous times and many more than was necessary to kill. Fourthly there was a sexual element to the killings. Finally, the exhibits in the Bisset case showed that Robert Napper bore a striking resemblance to Colin Stagg.

Breaking off from reading the papers, I went up to my clerk and told him: 'This chap that Robin Murray & Co have asked me to defend, Robert Napper, he's the chap who killed Rachel Nickell.' If I had made the connection, why hadn't the police? It was a case with a long and sad history.

Napper had a profoundly disturbed background. His

mother, Pauline, had been a victim of domestic violence and while a young boy he had been treated by psychiatrists. Aged 12, he had been sexually abused by a family friend, after which his behaviour had caused his mother considerable concern. He had become obsessively tidy and withdrawn and spied upon his sister while she undressed.

When Napper was in his twenties he tried to commit suicide. He told his mother he had raped a woman on Plumstead Common and she alerted police. Having checked no such crimes had been reported, a desk sergeant took no further action. Eight weeks later a woman whose home backed onto Plumstead Common reported that she had been raped by a masked intruder who had entered her home brandishing a Stanley knife. The police still did not interview Napper.

They also did not interview Napper when an extremely violent man raped three women in separate attacks on Green Chain Walk, Eltham, in mid-1992. A few weeks later Rachel Nickell was murdered on Wimbledon Common in another vicious, sexually-motivated attack.

In October 1992, when Napper began stalking a civilian worker at Plumstead police station the police finally acted and searched Napper's bedsit. They found a .22 pistol, 244 bullets, knives and a crossbow along with diaries and hand-drawn maps. Pages of an A-Z streetmap covering Plumstead, Eltham and Woolwich were marked with a series of dots and dashes. Napper was jailed for eight weeks.

A few months later police found a tin bearing Napper's fingerprints on Winn's Common. Inside was a Mauser handgun. Napper was not rearrested.

Paul Britton worked on the Green Chain Walks rapes inquiry as well as on the Nickell murder, but he did not make a link between these two crimes both in areas of south London, on or adjacent to common land and just a few miles apart. Napper remained at large and, instead, in August 1993, police charged Colin Stagg with Rachel Nickell's murder.

After all this, in November 1993, Samantha and Jazmine Bisset were murdered. In May 1994, detectives found DNA linking Napper to the Green Chain cases and then to the Bisset murder. Napper was charged with the murders of the Bissets – and quickly transferred to Broadmoor High Security Hospital in Berkshire, diagnosed with paranoid schizophrenia and Asperger's syndrome.

It was in the odd confines of Broadmoor that I saw him for the first time, with his solicitor Richard Atkinson. Broadmoor was ringed by a wall umpteen metres high. Inside, however, it didn't give the impression of being a very high-security establishment. Patients were wandering around comparatively free and the atmosphere was relaxed and even rather pleasant.

Despite this, I was acutely aware that I was in a dangerous environment. Napper's ward contained patients who had been convicted of appalling crimes. We were chaperoned by the nursing staff until we got to the room where the consultation was due to take place but, once there, they all promptly pushed off and left us alone with Napper to get on with it.

It didn't take me long to establish that Napper was completely mad. He wasn't physically intimidating in the least. He was such a puny little thing, almost weedy. He would talk about things very randomly. I remember him suddenly describe being visited by a member of the Royal Family with such sincerity that I almost had to pinch myself to remind myself that he was delusional.

The evidence against him on the Bisset murders was overwhelming. He had obviously done it — there was no doubt — but he was still entitled to legal representation. However, it was quite impossible to have a sensible dialogue with him. I think he understood who I was but he had no understanding of the issues in the case. He thought it was all down to 'aliens'.

I don't think he was pretending. His belief that extra-terrestrial life was controlling him was borne out by written documents found in his flat by the police after his arrest. He wanted to plead not guilty, on the basis that it was the aliens who should have been in the dock.

When he first appeared before a magistrates court there was a debate as to whether he was insane, but in the end the prosecution doctors insisted that he was fit to plead because they could understand what he was saying, even though he was operating on a completely different wavelength to everyone else. Although he was suffering from delusions, they maintained that he knew perfectly well what he was doing. At the time, unless a defendant instructed me to say so, I couldn't ask the court to decide whether they were unfit to enter a plea. In such circumstances, the defendant would invariably say: 'There's nothing wrong with me, what are you on about? I'm the only sane person here!' So it was with Napper.

The obvious route for me was to get Napper to admit to the manslaughter of Samantha and Jazmine on the grounds of diminished responsibility. He comfortably fitted all of the criteria and, fortunately on this, the prosecution doctors agreed with our experts, but recognising that something is the best outcome and getting your client to agree to it are two different things.

After several days of persuasion, Napper did finally agree to plead guilty to manslaughter. He physically had to sign a document in the cells of the Old Bailey in October 1995 prior to appearing before the judge, Sir Anthony Hooper. From Napper's point of view the plea meant that he could go straight back to Broadmoor, where he was quite content.

I had to present arguments in Napper's favour before sentencing. Where a person has pleaded guilty or been found guilty of an offence, his lawyer may offer mitigation — facts which are in the defendant's favour and which may reduce their sentence. But it was a mere formality with Napper. All I could really say was that he was clearly very ill. It was just for the record because whatever I said could not affect the sentence.

Napper was made the subject of an indefinite Hospital Order. He showed no reaction or emotion in court at all. He will only be released with the express permission of the Home Secretary. Decades into the future when everyone has forgotten who he is, which Home Secretary will allow him to be released? Why would they take the risk?

Two months after Napper pleaded guilty to the Bisset murders, police interviewed him about the murder of Rachel Nickell. He vehemently denied any responsibility.

By the time I had realised that the cases were likely to be connected, Colin Stagg had been found not guilty and Napper was already in custody for the murders of Jazmine and Samantha Bisset and — given the fingerprint evidence — likely to be so for the rest of his life. Sharing my suspicions with the police probably wouldn't have carried any weight and not doing so did not result in any danger to the public. At the end of the day, my suspicions were just that: suspicions.

What happened with the Rachel Nickell inquiry? In 2002 the Metropolitan Police carried out a 'Cold Case Review', when a team of detectives re-examined all the evidence and possible links to other unsolved crimes. They also subjected the original physical evidence to the latest DNA techniques. After 18 months of tests, the police identified a male DNA profile on Ms Nickell's clothing which didn't belong to her partner, her young son or to Colin Stagg. At the time it was enough to rule out certain suspects, but not enough to identify her killer. Four years later further advances in mitochondrial DNA technology matched the sample to Napper. He was finally charged with Ms Nickell's murder in 2007, 15 years after her untimely death.

At the Old Bailey in 2008, Napper eventually admitted her manslaughter on the grounds of diminished responsibility. I could not represent him then because my defence of Colin Stagg would have been a conflict of interest.

I was pleased for Ms Nickell's family that her killer had finally been identified. Colin eventually received a public apology from the Metropolitan Police and, later, some damages to compensate him for the police conduct. Detectives working on the Green Chain Walk cases have identified attacks on 86 women. Napper, still incarcerated in Broadmoor, has only admitted cases where the forensic evidence is overwhelming.

Unfortunately, sometimes the police arrest the wrong man, and that allows the guilty man to commit more crimes. In Napper's case there was no evidence linking him to Ms Nickell's murder when the police first investigated the crime. Only later advances in forensic evidence proved his guilt. But at the time detectives had convinced themselves that Colin Stagg was the Wimbledon killer and so had stopped looking for other suspects.

CHAPTER FOUR

Ronnie Trott, pupil master

~

After passing the Bar Finals, the final step for any law student intent on becoming a practising barrister is to undertake a pupillage, which is a sort of apprenticeship where you spend a year in chambers under the tutelage of a senior barrister before, hopefully, striking out on your own.

Frustratingly, for the first six months of a pupillage you cannot appear in court to represent anybody yourself and have to shadow your pupil supervisor, who instructs you on how to conduct yourself in court, on the ethics of the profession, and your duties and obligations as a barrister. In the second six months of pupillage you can appear in court on your own and for the first time are let loose on the public.

After the Bar Council exams most aspiring advocates planned to take the summer off and start their pupillage in September or October. I wanted to start straight away. But there was just one difficulty: actually getting a pupillage. By a stroke of luck, my parents knew a solicitor called Peter Laing of the law firm Fisher & Laing, who had arranged the leases for their two flower shops in Westcliff and Leigh-on-Sea. My father decided to have a word with Peter and ask him if he knew a barrister who might accept me for a pupillage. Luckily, he was friendly with a barrister called Ronnie Trott and agreed to ask him if he would take me as a pupil. I was summoned to Ronnie's house in Brentwood, Essex, where I spent the evening with him and his glamorous wife, Glenna.

There was a lot riding on my visit to the Trott residence that night. Obtaining pupillage is more formal these days, with law students undergoing interviews and aptitude tests, but at least they know what's going to happen. I hadn't got the faintest idea when I turned up at the Trotts'. Once Ronnie had introduced me to Glenna, a former dancer, he wanted to know all about my background. Then he talked about the work he did and showed me some papers from a murder case he was doing, which I found very exciting. He was a very likeable and approachable man. At the end of the evening he said 'Alright you're in. When do you want to start?'

So it was that in May 1972 Ronnie became my pupil master. My parents had to pay him 100 guineas, which was the fee for a pupillage (100 pounds to Ronnie and 10 pounds to his clerk.) Ronnie took on another pupil that year, a retired police chief inspector called Colin Woodford, who became a close friend and was later appointed a judge at Norwich Crown Court. Tragically, Colin was killed in a road accident on his way to court early in his judicial career.

Ronnie was one of about 18 barristers in 3 Hare Court, a chambers in the Inns of Court situated between Fleet Street and the Embankment. Barristers' offices are called 'chambers' for historic reasons and in the 1970s were positively Dickensian, with cramped rooms, poor visitor facilities and no central heating.

Ronnie wasn't a typical barrister. He was the antithesis of everything I thought a barrister would be. He was short, wiry and had a lot of curious prejudices. He didn't believe in dentists and only had about four teeth. He was a vegetarian and a teetotaller and used to smoke roll-up cigarettes in a cigarette holder. He had previously worked as an engineer or scientist for Marconi. The bar was his second career and, like me, he hadn't been to public school. He was very down to earth.

Starting pupillage was tremendously exciting. I had watched proceedings from the public gallery of the Old Bailey and Bristol Assizes, but I had never actually witnessed a case from the well of a court. I vividly remember my first day as a pupil, as part of a privately-funded defence team for a woman charged with cheque fraud. Ronnie was being led by Michael Eastham, a Queen's Counsel, a more senior barrister. QCs generally appear in more serious cases and can command higher fees than an ordinary barrister. As I would learn in due course becoming one is not easy.

The case was held in an elegant townhouse in St James's Square, in the former home of Lady Astor, who was the first woman to take her seat in the House of Commons. (She had left her house to the nation and in those days London was short of courts). The case was adjourned on day one and the defendant's husband took us all off to Fortnum & Mason for lunch, which I thought tremendously grand. I remember thinking: 'I could live with 12 months of this!' It was the last free lunch I had for years.

Michael and Ronnie won the trial. For me it was a case of watching and learning. I was more interested in how the barristers behaved in front of the court than in the legalities of the case; Michael was very distinguished and went on to become a High Court judge. My first court case simply reinforced to me that the courts were where I wanted to work.

For most of the first six months of my pupillage Ronnie was junior to Barry Hudson, another QC, in a gargantuan fraud case. No court room at the Old Bailey was big enough to hold the case so it was held in the council chamber at Middlesex Guildhall, opposite the Houses of Parliament. Several MPs were among the barristers defending 10 people accused of obtaining credit to buy goods which they sold on without paying for them. It was a 'buy long, sell short' scam. Even though I wasn't taking an active part in the proceedings I could wear my wig and gown in court; I felt that my legal career had truly begun.

Outside of court I was given homework, such as drafting divorce papers which would then be marked. I was asked to read up on Ronnie's pending cases so we could discuss them at court, and I had to do some research. I found the pupillage exciting but as I approached the end of my first six months I became keen to appear in a case in my own right.

That moment came at a murder committal on 4 December 1972, in the case of R v Nolan & Others[2] at Wallington Magistrates Court in Surrey. Another barrister was scheduled to make a 'no case to answer' submission on behalf of one of my client's co-accused. I was under strict instructions to act only as an observer. Somewhat gallingly, the day before the hearing Ronnie took me aside and told me: 'Under no circumstances do anything or ask any questions.' In the event the 'no case' submission failed. To this date I haven't received my £10 fee from the instructing solicitors, Sampsons. (If they're reading this, it's never too late to make amends).

The day after my enforced silence at Wallington I was again brought down to earth with a bump. I was dispatched to Dartford Juvenile Court in Kent to defend a boy accused of breaking a window at the back of a hall. The case against him was that he happened to be in the area at the time with a 'guilty' look on his face and no alibi. He was convicted, quite against the weight of the

2 *R being Regina, ie The Queen, versus the defendants*

evidence in my view. It was a glorious failure. But I was quite philosophical and not at all deterred. And I was going to have to get used to it; statistically most criminal cases end with a conviction. On a happier note my fee for a day in court was £8. A handsome reward to my mind, and far better than the £20-a-week I earned for the Co-op bread round in Westcliff-on-Sea. There would be more cases, sometimes two in the same day.

A lot of solicitors would send work into chambers and in those days you wouldn't always be paid for them, but they would brief chambers on other cases that you would get paid for. Back in those days some solicitors worked on the basis that if they were going to give big cases to a set (a group of barristers sharing the same offices) then the set could do the smaller ones for nothing. The first time I actually got paid was when I received £12 for Police v Clarke at Marlborough Street Magistrates Court one morning in January 1973. That afternoon I received £7 for doing a rent tribunal case at Barnet & Camden Rent Tribunal.

Sometimes I would do eight or ten different cases in a day. Many would be completely formal hearings at magistrates courts for defendants who had been remanded in custody and were waiting for their cases to be sent to the higher court. (In those days, defendants in custody had to come before a magistrate every week, which was a waste of court time).

I would also do very minor summary trials at Camberwell Green Juvenile Court, typically for boys aged 14 to 16 who were in trouble for burglary, fighting or shoplifting — and at other magistrates courts dotted around London.

Every morning Bow Street Magistrates Court in central London processed the people arrested in the West End the night before — street girls and disreputable-looking drunks, some of whom would have a dinner jacket and bow tie. Certain solicitors would slip a few pounds to the press to go and have a cup of coffee when their client came in so that their case wouldn't get in the papers.

Cheques were starting to come into Ronnie Trott's chambers, 3 Hare Court, with my name on them: I earned £12 in March 1973 and £131 the following month. The money seemed to go as quickly as it came, a lot of it on drinks after court. We would go to the Cock Tavern in Fleet Street or the Devereux just off the Strand, the haunts of lawyers and newspaper reporters.

I was also starting to freelance. I joined the Bar Mess at the Old Bailey, where less serious prosecutions were doled out from a rota called the 'Soup List.' I had some five or six-day prosecutions at the Bailey thanks to the Soup List.

At the end of my pupillage I applied to join 3 Hare Court as a tenant. Getting a tenancy would make me a fully-fledged practising barrister in my own right. Tenants effectively have a job for life. Wrenchingly, I wasn't taken on, but my good friend and co-pupil Colin Woodford got the nod from the head of chambers, Eric Myers, instead. I then became something of an embarrassment in legal circles: a 'squatter'. A squatter is a barrister without a tenancy who loiters around chambers trying not to get in the way, feeding off scraps of work that nobody else wants to do. Squatters are a part of the wider chambers family, but on the very periphery. At 3 Hare Court four of us were in this precarious situation — myself, Peter Corrigan, Bruce Coleman and Keith McLaughlin. People were perfectly friendly and polite but we weren't regarded as a part of the chambers family. We didn't tend to receive invitations to social events. We would go out with each other to the pub, but we would be drinking halves because we couldn't afford pints.

Despite being disappointed at missing out on a tenancy I wasn't overly worried. I was sure something would turn up. Eventually, however, 3 Hare Court told me and my three fellow squatters that it was time for us to move on and we set up in a ramshackle office in rented rooms around the corner in Pump Court. We were still being unofficially 'clerked' through 3 Hare Court and somehow making ends meet, but they were uncertain times.

Fortunately, in one of the spasmodic eruptions in London's legal world, several barristers broke away from 3 Hare Court to form their own chambers. In their absence I secured a tenancy at 3 Hare Court, two fellow squatters found tenancies elsewhere and the fourth found employment with H.M. Customs and Excise. Finally, I was a proper barrister. Now it was time to take on some bigger cases.

CHAPTER FIVE

Case 3
The Chillenden Murders

~

Like most defence barristers I usually go into court on the first day of a case truly believing I have at least a fighting chance of winning it. But sometimes no matter how thin a prosecution case is, no matter how many holes you can blow in it, no matter how succinct and plausible your final address, the jury seem intent on returning a guilty verdict. One such case where I ended up feeling the odds were stacked against me from the start was that of Michael Stone, the man currently serving life in prison for the murder of a mother and daughter on a quiet country lane in Chillenden, Kent, on 9 July 1996, and the attempted murder of her other daughter.

Dr Lin Russell, 45, Josie, nine, and Megan, six, were

walking home from a swimming gala with their dog Lucy when a car passed them. As they continued down the lane they noticed the car was parked across the track. As they approached, the driver got out brandishing a hammer, and demanded money from them. Terrified, Dr Russell explained that she had left her purse at home and offered to go back to the house with him to get him the money, but he refused. In a panic Dr Russell told Josie to run to the nearest house to get help, but the man grabbed her before she could move and hit her with the hammer. He then walked all three members of the family into a dense copse where he tied them up with strips torn from Josie's blue swimming towel, a bootlace, and a pair of tights, before launching a frenzied attack during which he inflicted numerous hammer blows on each of them and killed their dog.

About half an hour later a man was spotted a mile away from the scene in an agitated state. He was seen to drop a string bag containing the bloodied towel strips before making off. When police arrived, they believed Dr Russell and both of her daughters were dead, but the doctor called out to certify the deaths discovered that Josie was still alive, just. She was taken to King's College Hospital in London where doctors saved her life. Amazingly, she made a full recovery and went on to lead something approaching a normal life with her father.

The brutality and pointlessness of the attack shocked the nation and received intense media coverage, but, as with the murder of Rachel Nickell, nearly a year passed before police found their prime suspect. Michael Stone was an unemployed man who lived 40 miles from the killings. He was arrested in July 1997 and charged with the murders of Lin and Megan Russell and the attempted murder of Josie. To Kent Police Stone looked like the kind of person who might have committed such a hideous attack. He was a drug addict with a chaotic lifestyle who had serious convictions including some for violence dating back to 1972.

Stone's childhood was blighted. He had witnessed domestic violence and was put in local authority care, where he was sexually and physically abused. When he left care he moved to Gillingham and became a heroin addict. In 1981 he had been jailed for two years for attacking a man with a hammer during a robbery. Two years later he was sentenced to four-and-a-half years for two counts of actual bodily harm after stabbing a sleeping 'friend' in the chest, and in 1987 he was sentenced to 10 years for two armed robberies. After his release in 1993, he had managed to avoid arrest, despite needing to inject heroin five times a day. As well as having a drink problem, he had a personality disorder for which he was receiving psychiatric treatment. Stone was a deeply troubled individual.

However, just like Colin Stagg in the Wimbledon Common case, it was clear from reading the prosecution files that there was virtually no evidence against him. Indeed, the case against him appeared to be based on the fact that he looked like the sort of person who might be responsible. There was some dispute about whether he was or wasn't in the area at the time of the killings, but it was all quite unclear. Astonishingly, there was no forensic evidence linking him to the killings despite the carnage at the scene. With the chaotic lifestyle he was leading it was difficult to see how he could have disposed of his bloody clothes without anybody seeing him. He didn't seem to have any conceivable motive to kill the Russells. The evidence was extremely suspect. I found it difficult to see how the Crown Prosecution Service could justify charging him.

As usual in murder cases, I saw a lot of Stone while he was on remand at a number of different prisons in the south of England, including for a time at Canterbury Prison, while he was waiting for his trial. By the time I met him he had got off drugs. Although he obviously had mental health problems, he was quite intelligent and rational, albeit a little manipulative. People who have had his problems can behave like that. He would sometimes try to play people off against each other. It was like a game for him. He was perfectly co-operative towards me because I was trying to secure him a not guilty verdict.

His prospects worsened when two remand prisoners came forward separately to say that he had confessed to them that he had carried out the murders. One claimed Stone had personally told him that he was the killer and the other claimed to have overheard him confessing through the pipework running along the wall between their neighbouring cells.

Suddenly the Crown Prosecution Service had a real case, but prisoner-to-prisoner confessions are notoriously difficult for prosecutors. Convicts know that they can benefit from testifying against people accused of very serious crimes. Such prison 'confessions' carry more weight when the defendant has revealed an aspect of a case known only to the perpetrator and the police, rather than something reported by the media. That didn't apply in this instance, although some of what one of the men claimed Stone had said would have required some effort to acquire and memorise.

We weren't contemplating calling Stone as a witness when his trial began at Maidstone Crown Court in 1998. I don't think he could have stood the pressure. His mental health problems would have made it difficult for him to give evidence and the prosecution would have found him easy to rattle. In a sense there was no need for him to take the stand because there was hardly any evidence against him. I explained his decision not to give evidence to the jury on the basis that he could do nothing more than reiterate what he had said throughout all his police interviews — that he wasn't responsible for the killings. He hadn't given 'no comment' interviews to the police. He had denied involvement all along. There was no evidence he did it. There was nothing more he could add.

Anne Rafferty QC, for the Crown, was a formidable

opponent but I didn't see how she could gain a conviction on such flimsy evidence. In his summing up the trial judge, Mr Justice Ian Kennedy, effectively told the jury that if they had any doubt concerning the prison confessions then the other evidence against Stone wasn't enough to return a guilty verdict. Much to my disappointment he was convicted, by a majority verdict of 10-2.

When I saw him later in the cells, Stone didn't show any emotion, but maintained his protestations of innocence. Within 48 hours one of the prisoners who had given evidence against him admitted to a national newspaper that he had made it all up. It was clear that we now had strong grounds to appeal the conviction. One of the prosecution's main witnesses had falsely alleged that Stone had confessed and the jury had been misled.

At the Court of Appeal, the new prosecuting barrister, Nigel Sweeney QC (Anne Rafferty had become a High Court judge) more or less admitted the conviction was difficult to maintain, but insisted there should be a re-trial. It was very difficult to argue against a retrial, though I tried, pointing out that Stone had received plenty of bad publicity which would make it difficult for him to get a fair hearing. I failed to convince the court.

The re-trial at Nottingham Crown Court in 2001 hinged entirely on the evidence of a single ex-prisoner, Damian Daley, who claimed to have overheard Stone confessing to the killings through the pipework running between their adjoining cells on C Wing of Canterbury Prison.

My junior and I decided to test Daley's claims that you could hear from one cell to another by visiting the jail. We established that you had to make quite a din before the other person could hear you and picking out individual words was difficult. But we were also told that prisoners often dug away the brick material from around the pipes which connected the cells to conceal contraband. These crevices were filled in again when the prison authorities discovered them, but some prisoners maintained you could hear what was said in adjoining cells before the repairs were made. It simply wasn't possible to know what state the walls had been in at the time of the alleged overheard confession. The jury were taken to the relevant cell while a forensics officer read out a passage from *Harry Potter and the Goblet of Fire* from a neighbouring cell.

When I cross-examined Daley, he insisted he had been able to hear a confession from Stone. 'I lie to get by in life. I'm a crook. That's what crooks do. They beg, borrow, steal and lie however they can to get by,' Daley, a heroin addict and reputedly a police informant, told me. 'But if you were to say to me now, "Are you lying?" I would say, "No, I am not".'

Quite simply, the jury had to decide which man to believe.[3] Nothing rivals the tension that builds in a courtroom of a major criminal trial in the moments before the

---

3 Damian Daley was jailed for life in 2014 for his part in the murder of a drug dealer. He had pleaded not guilty to the offence at his trial

jury foreman returns the verdict. It's greater than anything a playgoer experiences in a West End theatre, no matter who's on stage. In a court with 150 to 200 people you can hear a pin drop. It's a highly emotional time, not just for the defendant and their immediate family but also for the legal team working with them. Unfortunately, Michael Stone was again convicted, by a majority verdict of 10-2.

There was still absolutely no forensic evidence against Stone, but jurors are under a lot of psychological pressure to convict in cases where there have been such heinous crimes. A part of everybody wants the defendant to be guilty, because if he is guilty it means the police have done their job and caught the criminal; an evil man has been put behind bars and we can all sleep safer in our beds. The alternative is unthinkable — that there's a dangerous killer on the loose.

Clearly Stone could have done it. I genuinely don't know one way or the other whether he did. But he has always maintained his innocence and in my opinion the evidence against him is not convincing.

CHAPTER SIX

Learning how to fight a case

~

During the 1970s and early 1980s I would regularly defend clients accused of robbery, burglary and assault. In the morning I would drive to a Crown Court, have a conference with my client, appear in court all day, and in the evening drive to prison or chambers for conferences on pending cases. Occasionally I would be a junior barrister in a more serious case. I did none of the questioning but helped the QC prepare the case, took notes of the evidence in court and was a general dogsbody liaising with the solicitor.

As the seriousness of my cases increased at the start of the 1980s, I defended 'traditional' armed robbers, who would walk into high street banks with a sawn-off shotgun or ambush security vans. Many were old school criminals who had their own curious code: they thought robbing banks was a perfectly legitimate exercise, but anything to do with children or women was heinous and deserved condign punishment.

I also defended dozens of people accused of murder: shootings, stabbings and stranglings. Some busy solicitors in south London probably sent me all their murder cases.

Unsurprisingly, I found that the reality of being a barrister was dramatically unlike the common image of a dashing advocate constantly jumping to his feet to question a witness or address a jury with a passionate closing speech. Far less time was spent on spiky cross-examination and far more wading through vast amounts of paperwork.

And what I learnt was always to start by looking at the prosecution case against my client. To my surprise, many defence barristers started with the defence, looking at everything from the client's perspective and trying to establish 'What are we saying? What is our client saying?' My approach was to forget about that and first to see what the other side was saying and whether they could actually establish what they were alleging. I would pretend for a moment that I was the prosecutor and work out what they would be doing to try to prove the case and how, then look at it the other way around and try to spot the pitfalls in their approach.

I learnt to speed read, scanning a file of papers to identify those passages I needed to revisit. When I reached important witnesses I read their evidence again and again, thinking about it all the time. Often, the thinking was as important as the reading.

I nearly always visited the scene of a murder to understand the evidence and to speak more authoritatively in court. There was also the possibility that I would uncover some aspect of the evidence that could be challenged. Prior to Colin Stagg's trial, I visited the scene of the murder on Wimbledon Common and stumbled across the prosecution barrister doing exactly the same thing.

Details can be important in a case, so I always prepared properly. When questioning witnesses, I would plot out my questions extremely carefully beforehand. I would decide upon a route through the witness's evidence, usually a chronological one. I would make notes on a notepad, marking down the relevant subjects with bullet points.

I found that real-life cases rarely proceeded like American and British court dramas, with their interminable interruptions from the public gallery, furious rows between the prosecution and defence counsel, irritable comments from the judges and last minute interventions from new witnesses.

First the prosecution would present its evidence, with its own witnesses. Then came 'half-time', when defence lawyers would sometimes ask the judge to end the case on the basis that the prosecution's evidence had failed to establish a case to answer either because the evidence had failed to prove one of the essential elements of the offence or that the evidence was so flawed that the case could not be safely left to a jury to decide. Assuming that was unsuccessful, the defence would presents its case, calling its own witnesses. During both the prosecution and defence phases, witnesses would be asked questions by their own side (examination in chief) and the opposing side (cross-examination).

Ordinarily, the factual evidence would be known to all parties prior to a case. However, sometimes things would emerge in cross-examination that nobody had anticipated, not even your opponent. During my early years, I was involved in a case where a number of defendants were charged with blackmail for trying to extort cash from a man who had asked them to collect a debt. All of them were known to the authorities.

Not content with simply recovering what was owed for their client, these men set about duping him into paying them more money by hatching an elaborate hoax. They claimed that a number of them had been seriously injured while collecting the debt and that two had suffered broken arms and another a cracked skull. The upshot was that they wanted more money from him to recompense them for the injuries.

To back up their story they took the client somewhere in the East End where they had set up a bogus casualty ward. It was like something out of *Carry On Doctor*, with some rickety beds, a woman in a matron's uniform and people lying around with their arms in plaster. Eventually the client went to the police who raided the home of one of the defendants where they rather inconveniently found a plastercast for his arm in the fridge. By the time the matter came to trial the defence case was that the hospital story had all been made up by their client and that the plastercast was a prop which the man had worn for a fancy dress party.

Dozens of photographs were produced as evidence of this party, which undoubtedly did take place, although almost certainly after the defendant's arrest and release on bail, featuring him with his arm in plaster, jiggling with his wife and dancing around with Marie Antoinette, Little Bo Peep and various others. In good old East End tradition dozens of people who claimed to have been at the party came along to give evidence in his support, swearing on oath that he had been present and that he had his arm in a fake plastercast. All very well until the prosecution called an expert who revealed that the plastercast visible in the photographs taken at the party was wound around the arm in the opposite direction to the one found in the fridge.

The defence case was sunk. Sometimes it's the details that hold the key to a case.

CHAPTER SEVEN

Case 4
Helen Hodgson

~

I have great respect for police officers and the often very difficult job they do. But in the 1970s and 1980s every case seemed to centre on alleged confessions that defendants would immediately retract the moment they had been charged. What we called 'the verbals' became a legal sport. Very few people believed that professional criminals were overcome with a burning desire to confess the moment they were interviewed by two members of the Flying Squad, only to recant the moment they saw a solicitor two hours later. Detectives routinely denied a prisoner access to a solicitor, interviewed him when he was unrepresented, took no contemporaneous note of the interview, and made a short note afterwards recording a full confession.

Some cases became especially notorious, when the police were under pressure to catch the perpetrators of horrendous crimes. The Guildford Four and Birmingham Six were convicted in 1975 of carrying out Irish republican pub bombings in which a total of 26 people lost their lives. All 10 defendants were freed years later after new evidence emerged showing that confessions had been fabricated by police. When concerns about police treatment of suspects reached fever pitch, Margaret Thatcher's government introduced a far-reaching law, the Police and Criminal Evidence Act (PACE), which set much higher standards for police interviews and the gathering of evidence.

Among other things, PACE required police to make audio recordings of their interviews with suspects, which largely ended the fabrication of confessions. It also introduced a statutory right of a suspect held at a police station to see a solicitor. After PACE's introduction in 1985, the number of miscarriages of justice because of false confessions fell dramatically.

Occasionally, however, cases still went wrong. One involved Cherie McGovern, a young woman with learning difficulties living in south London. McGovern was 19 when she was arrested by the police at 7am on 17 November 1987. She and three others were charged with taking part in the savage killing of a 21-year-old woman, Helen Hodgson, in Charlton. There was an element of communal living in the relationships between the parties. Without being too unkind, the good Lord had not been generous with brain cells with any of them. According to the story bolted together by detectives later, one of the women, Agnes Carpenter, had wanted a third child after being sterilised following the first two. She and her husband Ian allegedly approached Helen Hodgson, who agreed to bear them a surrogate and moved in with them. However, Mrs Carpenter soon become jealous at her husband's increasing desire to spend time with Ms Hodgson. She then purportedly suggested to Cherie McGovern, a friend of hers, Cherie's brother George and Cherie's common-law husband, Andy Watkinson, that they do away with Ms Hodgson — in exchange for the right to order goods free from the Carpenters' mail order catalogue. On 16 November 1987, Ms Hodgson was stabbed and hit around the head with a frying pan. She was asphyxiated by string, the pulling of a rope around her neck, and quick-setting glue being pushed into her lips and nostrils. While she was still alive, she was thrown into the Thames and drowned. Her disappearance was soon reported to police.

When it came to the trial at the Old Bailey in November 1988, I quickly identified that the only evidence against the heavily pregnant Cherie McGovern was her supposed 'confession'. There was no forensic evidence against her. Indeed, the only evidence against all of the defendants was what they had each said about themselves and the others: there were no other witnesses as to what had happened. I immediately focused on the confession and it became clear that what had gone on inside the police station had been highly unsatisfactory. Before the interview had begun, Cherie McGovern had been vomiting. At the start of the interview she could not understand the caution given to her until it had been broken down into much simpler language. (McGovern had an IQ of 71 and was compared by a psychologist to a 10-year-old child.) During the interview, she had difficulty following the questions and had sobbed uncontrollably. She allegedly confessed to the killing. But, contrary to the code of conduct brought in by PACE three years earlier, her interview was not tape recorded, nor had the police made any contemporaneous notes. McGovern had asked for a solicitor but her request had been unlawfully denied. The police had broken pretty much every rule in the book.

A second interview was conducted the following day, apparently within the rules. At this interview, at which a solicitor was present, Cherie McGovern confessed to playing a part in Ms Hodgson's death.

Before the jury was sworn I made legal representations to the judge with a view to excluding the confession, because the rules had been broken and the police could not prove that it had been made properly. If successful, the application would have resulted in McGovern's immediate acquittal on the grounds that she had no case to answer. Unfortunately, the trial judge, His Honour Richard Lowry QC allowed the evidence to be admitted. He ruled that the breaches of PACE were not such that it ought to result in the confession being ruled inadmissible. The jury subsequently convicted Cherie McGovern of manslaughter on the grounds of diminished responsibility. She was given 10 years in a young offenders' institution. All the other defendants were convicted of murder.

In his evidence, the police officer who interviewed Cherie McGovern said he had not realised that she had asked for a solicitor. When dealing with the first interview, he said:

> The lady didn't understand all the questions. She didn't even know why she was in the police station. In the last part of the interview she was crying; she was clearly upset; she was crying heavily. Yes, I carried on questioning her. She was not offered a break to compose herself, not even a glass of water. I never offered her a solicitor until she confessed.

I knew I had strong grounds of appeal. Unlike the Crown Court, where cases of murder are decided by jurors, judges decide appeals.

There were four reasons why the confession obtained in the first interview was unreliable. The police had unlawfully denied McGovern access to a solicitor, no contemporaneous note was kept of the interview, she was clearly vulnerable and, finally, she had been physically sick in her cell immediately before the interview.

I argued before the Court of Appeal that the second interview had taken place as a direct consequence of the first, and that if her solicitor had been made properly aware of the circumstances of how that interview had taken place, he would have realised the 'confession' should have been excluded and would have advised her to remain silent. The Court of Appeal agreed that the first interview was inadmissible because it had broken the rules, and that — consequently — the second interview was, too.

The judges explained:

> One cannot refrain from emphasising that when an accused person has made a series of admissions as to his or her complicity in a crime at a first interview, the very fact that those admissions have been made are likely to have an effect upon her during the course of the second interview. If accordingly, it be held, as it is held here, that the first interview was in breach of section 78 and the Code it seems to us that the subsequent interview must be similarly tainted.

The Court of Appeal quashed the conviction, ruling that the trial judge was wrong not to exclude the confession evidence, explaining that the second interview had been 'tainted by the illegality of the first'. The judges remarked: 'Whether it is a satisfactory consequence that a confession which was admitted to be a true account of the appellant's participation in this wicked and terrible killing should be excluded because of the breaches of the Act and the [PACE] Code of Conduct is, no doubt, a matter for debate, but we are satisfied that is the effect in law.'

There are good reasons why the police should follow the rules and a failure to do so risks compromising an investigation. Over the years PACE has enhanced the professionalism of police officers. In my career this statute has done more than anything else to transform the evidence put before a jury.

CHAPTER EIGHT

Mutiny at 3 Hare Court

~

As I started attracting more and more criminal cases, I became more familiar with what, to most outsiders, may seem the strange inner workings of a barristers' chambers. When a client comes into a set for an interview, they may notice only the old buildings, or perhaps the wooden panelling, or the urbane manner and friendliness of the lawyer they are visiting. Inside, a working barrister must negotiate the undercurrents that swirl around the corridors. Chambers house rivalries, ambition and occasionally resentment.

When I joined 3 Hare Court as a pupil in 1972 it was a middle-ranking criminal set, doing perfectly well for its tenants but was not viewed as a 'first tier' chambers. The powerhouses in those days were 5 King's Bench Walk, 6 Kings Bench Walk, and Queen Elizabeth Buildings.

In many ways, 3 Hare Court was quite antiquated. It was an exclusively male preserve — the Head of Chambers wouldn't countenance the prospect of a female tenant – and there was no question of anyone from any ethnic minority being permitted to work there. The Head of Chambers and the senior clerk ran the place. There was a small token committee that was consulted over chambers' matters but it had no real power or influence. There was no constitution.

I realised 3 Hare Court's fortunes (and indeed every chambers' fortunes) were down in large part to its clerks. Without the clerks little would get achieved.

Clerks are the conduit between solicitors and barristers. Most importantly, they agree the fees a barrister will charge for representing a client. Clerks also collect those fees, fix conferences and agree court dates. In many ways the clerks are required to have a similar skill set to a broker in the City – they must be good with numbers, have sound judgement, an exceptional memory, and be able to make instant decisions. Sometimes a clerk has only minutes to decide whether to take on a large case, without being able to consult the barrister concerned.

In the 1970s, the senior clerks within legal chambers had a well-earned reputation for being heavy drinkers who spent an inordinate length of time out of the office swapping briefs with their opposite numbers and gossiping in the pubs dotted around Fleet Street. When the pubs closed at 3pm they would usually make their way down to the City Golf Club next to St Bride's Church where they would continue imbibing until the taverns reopened again at 5pm. Among this merry band of senior clerks was an individual whose liquid lunching exploits were legendary even among his peers — 3 Hare Court's very own Barry Welfare.

I and a few of the younger barristers felt that Barry's junior, John Grimmer, was doing most of the work in chambers so when our Head of Chambers, Eric Myers QC, announced he was retiring we seized the chance to shift the balance of power away from Barry. There was no provision for an election to the post of Head of Chambers back then and Eric's role was taken over by the chambers only other QC, Kenneth Machin.

Some of us with bigger practices – by then mine was one of the biggest even though I was still quite junior – went to see Kenneth and informed him that Eric's departure was the perfect opportunity to dispense with Barry and promote John to senior clerk.

Alas, Kenneth didn't seem to have the appetite for sacking his senior clerk and appeared very worried, perhaps with good reason, about the prospect of being sued by Barry for unfair dismissal. I and my fellow tenants Howard Godfrey, Charles Conway and Richard Haworth made it clear that there was no way we were prepared to carry on with Barry as senior clerk. Kenneth quickly decided to leave chambers and become a judge (he went on to sit at the Old Bailey and the International Criminal

Court), thereby avoiding any unpleasant consequences.

Faced with the continuing impasse, I and my three fellow conspirators — soon known as the 'Gang of Four' — announced that we would leave 3HC and set up our own chambers. We had already had a number of private meetings with John. He was far too diplomatic to say publicly that he didn't think he was getting a fair crack of the whip under Barry but he was only too happy to become our senior clerk. He was doing all the work and bringing in all the money.

We told everybody in chambers that we were leaving and issued an open invitation to our fellow tenants to join us if they wished. Almost all of them indicated they wanted to be a part of our new enterprise. Several older tenants, some of whom no longer needed to earn high fees, remained loyal to Barry.

With Eric retired and Kenneth heading for the bench, there was a power vacuum. Our group had no QC, and nor did the small band of Barry loyalists. In such circumstances the Inner Temple, which owned the building, would have to decide how many of the leases for its rooms would go to the 'Gang of Four' and our followers and how many to Barry's cohort.

We had previously told the barristers who wished to remain with Barry that we wanted three of the four leases and were happy for them to have the other one. But they insisted they should keep all four leases and that we would have to set up elsewhere. Much to our surprise the Inner

Temple ruled that we should have all four leases and found Barry's group new premises elsewhere in the Temple.

We were astonished. Looking back, the Inner Temple must have thought it would be rather unhealthy for us to share the same staircase with our former colleagues after falling out with them, and that as we had more tenants and were the bigger earners, we should prevail. It seemed to have been purely a business decision on its part to keep most of its tenants. Our 20 tenants could use all four leases whereas Barry and his loyalists didn't have the numbers to fill them. What's more, we were permitted to retain the name 3 Hare Court and the telephone number for the chambers, which was important at the time. Our former colleagues went to King's Bench Walk where they continued practising for a number of years, though they didn't prosper.

Many in the legal profession thought what we had done was daring, not to mention risky, but we were confident that as long as we could take John with us we couldn't go wrong. Suffice it to say, all these machinations were viewed by Barry's side as akin to a military-style coup on our part.

However, as a condition of allowing us to stay at 3 Hare Court the Inner Temple stipulated that our young set had to recruit a Queen's Counsel as Head of Chambers. Howard Godfrey had formerly done cases with a silk called Michael Lewis who specialised in personal injury litigation. While his line of work was much more respectable than our crime-rife operation, Michael was attracted by the amount of criminal cases that we could offer him, because silk work was rare in personal injury circles. We were able to show him what Kenneth Machin had earned and without wanting to make it sound like it was a purely commercial decision on his part he was satisfied that if he joined us he wouldn't starve. Michael accepted our invitation and was our Head of Chambers for a decade.

We established a proper chambers committee that made decisions democratically. We wanted tenants to be involved in making the decisions that affected their professional futures, such as taking on new employees that they would have to fund. We suggested that the original 'Gang of Four' join Michael on the committee and he agreed.

We also wanted to broaden the intake of barristers. It was 1984 and our chambers was approaching the 21st Century having appeared to have been stuck previously in the 19th Century.

CHAPTER NINE

Case 5
Waking the Dead in Belarus

~

When I first met Szymon Serafinowicz it was at my chambers at 3 Hare Court. He ambled in, his face veined with age, looking like an ordinary 84-year-old. His fluent English carried a trace of a Russian accent. Other than that, there was nothing special about him. He seemed to be a gentle old boy. I found him quite an engaging character; he could certainly keep me entertained. He had some marvellous first-hand stories about the Second World War and skirmishes with the partisans. He lived with his son in a mock-Tudor house in Banstead, Surrey.

According to the British state, he was also a war criminal. Days before our meeting, Serafinowicz had been accused of playing a significant role in the most heinous crime of the 20th Century. Now, more than 50 years after those events, he was facing trial in Britain for the Nazis' slaughter of the Jews 1,400 miles away in Belarus in the old Soviet Union.

It was the first prosecution in Britain for war crimes committed in Nazi-occupied Europe. My involvement in it came about because of a chance encounter at a snooker hall in Dorking. In 1995, Serafinowicz's son, also called Szymon, was a member of the same snooker hall as a lawyer who worked for Thompson Bowers, a firm of solicitors that regularly instructed my chambers. One evening Serafinowicz's son approached him and said: 'You're a lawyer, aren't you? My Dad's in a bit of bother. Is there any chance you could help him?'

The bit of bother was the 1991 War Crimes Act, a controversial Bill that passed into English law largely because of Margaret Thatcher, Prime Minister between 1979 and 1990, whose north London constituency had a large Jewish population. She became a passionate proponent of the legislation after learning that more than 350 suspected war criminals had fled to Britain after the Second World War. But every time she tried to enact the law (which gave the courts the jurisdiction to try suspected war criminals living in Britain for alleged crimes that took place abroad), she was blocked by the House of Lords. Members of the upper house felt strongly that the War Crimes Act was a case of 'far too little, far too late'. Many peers felt it would be impossible for anyone to have a fair trial more than 45 years after the event, that the evidence would always be unreliable, and that any such prosecutions should have been mounted in the 1940s and 50s. As it happened, I agreed with that sentiment, as did many in the legal profession. But Mrs Thatcher was not to be thwarted and invoked the Parliament Acts of 1911 and 1949 to force the law through.

Following its introduction in 1991, Scotland Yard set up a special unit to investigate British residents accused of committing atrocities in Nazi Germany or German-occupied territory during the Second World War. Technically a war crime is an act that violates the international rules of war, which could mean rape or torture or kidnapping or even the destruction of property. In practice it often involves murder in the aggravated form of genocide, which is murder of a group of people identified by and murdered because of their race, religion or ethnicity which is what happened to the Jews during the Second World War.

Detectives at Scotland Yard had access to a wealth of historical data when drawing up their list of targets. The Simon Wiesenthal Centre in Los Angeles (named after the famous Austrian-born Nazi hunter who devoted his life to bringing war criminals to justice) had published its list of alleged war criminals living in Britain online in an attempt to shame Westminster into action.

Empowered by the new legislation, Scotland Yard and the Crown Prosecution Service established the criteria suspects must meet before they could be prosecuted. Chiefly, it was decided not to go after anyone who had only been in a supporting role. Only those individuals accused of killing or ordering killings were liable to arrest. Additionally, the CPS would only pursue cases where there was clear evidence identifying both a perpetrator and 'war crimes', rather than murders committed in the course of combat, for example in fighting the partisans.

By this time, the Iron Curtain had crumbled and the former USSR was rapidly disintegrating. For the first time since the end of the Second World War it became possible to obtain the evidence needed to support war crimes prosecutions in Eastern Europe. Belarus, sandwiched between Poland and Russia, won independence in 1991, the year the War Crimes Act became law.

The Simon Wiesenthal Centre had named Szymon Serafinowicz, the octogenarian who arrived at my chambers, as a war criminal. His case would plunge me deep into one the darkest episodes in the 20th Century. Serafinowicz had been a member of the Belarussian police force when Germany invaded Belarus in 1941. The Russians, under Stalin, had been a cruel occupying army in Belarus and when the Nazis invaded they were initially treated as liberators by many members of the indigenous population, including the police. After the Germans invaded Belarus, Jews were driven from their homes and confined — as elsewhere — in barbed wire ghettoes, as well as being forced to wear clothes blazoned with yellow stars. The 'Final Solution' was brutally enacted by the Nazis' Einsatzgruppen regiments, which moved from town to town and village to village executing all known Jews. Large pits would be dug outside each town or village and the Jewish population would be herded there at gunpoint and shot, before their bodies were tossed into the abyss and covered with soil.

Officers of the puppet Belarussian police force were deployed in two ways — firstly, they guarded the route to the pit to make sure that nobody escaped during the death marches, and secondly, as the Einsatzgruppen moved on to 'cleanse' the next settlement, they executed any stragglers who had managed to avoid the cull.

Serafinowicz was the Belarussian police commander in the small town of Mir. He somehow managed to engineer himself a reason to be away from Mir on the day the Einsatzgruppen massacred the town's Jews, though he would have been responsible for deploying his officers, who were present. Instead, he was charged with four counts of murdering Jews in 1941 during the so-called mopping up operations conducted by the Belarussian police on Nazi orders. By the time the Nazi death squads got to Mir quite a number of the town's Jews, having got word of the impending round-up, had fled into the forests or hidden under the floorboards of their houses. As a result quite a few survived the massacre. When they later discarded their yellow-starred clothing they believed they were safe, because the Nazis had no way of knowing whether they were Jewish or not. But they were unaware the local police had been enlisted to identify any Jews left after the massacre and eliminate them. Amazingly, some lived to tell the tale.

Survivors remained hidden in the forests for three years, many joining existing partisan groups of communist sympathisers who had escaped the Nazis and some forming their own partisan groups. Others concealed themselves in the weave of ordinary life. One young Jewish man was taken into the local convent by the nuns, who hid him for the rest of the war. He ended up converting to Catholicism and becoming a monk. Incredibly another young Jew got a job working in a stables for some German officers, looking after their horses. When he was eventually exposed he was put in a cell in readiness to be shot, but one officer took pity on him and left the door unlocked so he could escape. Another Jewish man who was herded to the death pits toppled in unscathed as everyone around him was cut to shreds by machine gun fire. Later that night he dug himself out from under the dead bodies. He survived the war.

Scotland Yard detectives travelled to Mir and surrounding villages, interviewing inhabitants who answered their call for information about war crimes. Serafinowicz was duly charged and the case was due to be heard in the magistrates court where a professional magistrate would decide if there was sufficient evidence to send the case to the Crown Court for trial The prosecution instructed a Queen's Counsel and two junior counsel and Serafinowicz was granted Legal Aid to hire one Queen's Counsel to act for him. Thompson Bowers' first barrister, Michael Levy, stood aside and recommended me and I was appointed to defend Serafinowicz at the committal proceedings.

Usually committal proceedings lasted only a few days, but this ground-breaking prosecution came with a vast amount of paperwork and the proceedings were scheduled to last for weeks. The prosecution had a silk (a QC) and two juniors for the committal.

Under the normal rules, Legal Aid would fund a silk or a junior for the defence at a committal, but not both. However, the normal rules had not been designed for a case like this. For the first and only time in my career, I wrote to the government minister with responsibility for the courts, the Lord Chancellor, asking if there was anything he could do. Lord Mackay of Clashfern wrote back saying 'Yes, and I've organised it.' His budget for 'exceptional situations' would fund a junior. This allowed me to re-engage Michael, who is Jewish. So it came to be that a Jewish barrister helped to defend a man accused of murdering Jews. (Yet another example of lawyers representing clients regardless of the accusation they face, because they believe in the principle that everyone deserves a fair trial.)

To check out the prosecution case and gather our own evidence, Michael, our solicitor Nicholas Bowers and I travelled to Belarus. We had available to us all the evidence served by the prosecution, all the witness statements and exhibits they relied on to try to prove their case. The

Foreign Office and the Crown Prosecution Service had arranged permission from the authorities for us to do our work. As soon as we arrived in Belarus we were driven straight from the airport to meet their equivalent of our Attorney General. We had an interesting chat. He said he thought it was very odd that Britain allowed defendants in a trial to call their own witnesses. They didn't allow that in Belarus, he explained, because the witnesses might lie; instead, the prosecutor alone would question witnesses and ascertain whether they were lying. Rather than disagree with him, I remarked that our two countries clearly had different legal systems.

I don't think he quite understood what Queen's Counsel was and thought I might be related to Her Majesty. We exchanged presents. I had been tipped off that the item that would be most appreciated was a bottle of Scotch whisky. When I produced it, it disappeared pretty smartly into his desk. I also took him an Old Bailey tie, which seemed to be received with rather less enthusiasm. He warmly welcomed us on behalf of the state of Belarus and promised help. Unfortunately, it didn't materialise in a form we were able to recognise.

Our team flew to Belarus on several trips, the longest lasting a week. The prosecution had stayed in something rather vaguely described as 'bed and breakfast accommodation' near Mir but I declined the opportunity to do likewise when I heard what it was like. No restaurant in Mir was deemed safe, let alone desirable, whereas there was one half decent one in Minsk, the capital.

One of the first things we did was to hire a Belarussian interpreter at the hotel we stayed at. There were actually two interpreters at the hotel, both called Natascha. By way of identification we called them Fat Natascha and Thin Natascha. We ended up with Fat Natascha, who was great. I was asked how much we should pay her and I said: 'Well how much is the Legal Aid Board's approved rate for interpreters?' I suggested we pay her that. It was a fortune for her and transformed her life. She was able to move her mother into a new flat. I still have the Russian doll she gave me at the end of our last visit.

Like the Yard's team, we took evidence from people living in the Mir area. We had arranged for posters appealing for witnesses to go up before we arrived, explaining the allegations against Serafinowicz and our roles and asking anybody who could provide any evidence which showed him in a good light to come on a specific day to Mir Town Hall or one of the local village halls where we would record their accounts. Mir had only 2,000-3,000 residents and each of the surrounding villages about 200-300. It took days to get around the villages.

Perhaps as a result of our trip to the Government Legal Department, officers from the Belarussian equivalent of the KGB began 'helping' us. They weren't always helpful. We had trouble with our first man because he kept on interrupting the taking of witness statements, telling people not to say certain things. It was also pretty obvious that the phones in our hotel were tapped, albeit rather inefficiently. You could just hear these 'click, clack, clonk' noises on the line whenever you picked up the receiver. We used it to our advantage by complaining over the phone that our minder was making things so difficult for us we might have to come home, pointing out that the whole trial might have to be abandoned because of the obstruction we were facing. The following day he was mysteriously replaced by someone less meddlesome. I got the impression the Belarussian authorities were pro-prosecution. Though officially independent, Belarus was very much a Russian puppet which regarded the partisans (rather than Serafinowicz's allegedly pro-German policemen) to be the heroes of the war.

No-one who came to see us had anything to say about the actual allegations themselves. Some got het up when talking to us but the majority were blank-faced. Many were well into their 80s. Having survived a harsh climate in primitive conditions, they were not given to showing much emotion.

Sometimes we saw people in their houses. None of the witnesses we saw was Jewish. The prosecution spoke to some Jews who had been in Mir but they had left Belarus long ago. There was quite a bit of trouble in one village when we arrived to find a group of elderly ex-partisans who were trying to prevent the people who had answered our call from speaking to us. Many had pinned their medals on their jackets. Five decades after the events at the heart of the investigation passions still ran high.

Encouragingly for us some people spoke highly of Serafinowicz. One witness told how he had been responsible for saving a man's life by persuading the Germans not to shoot him and how the man's wife still prayed for him every day. Others said he would mediate with his German masters when they wanted to shoot people for helping the partisans, negotiating a reduction in the number of people to be shot.

I vividly remember one woman who said she wanted to speak to us, but felt too intimidated to do so in front of others and gave us her address instead. When we went out to her village to see her nothing appeared to have changed in 50 years. No western town would have been recognisable after that period of time but here the buildings were exactly as they were: single-storey wooden shacks without running water or electricity. The wealthier residents had wells with generators but the poorer ones still hauled the water up by hand. The ploughing was still being done by oxen with wooden ploughs. It was as if time had stood still.

Whatever had taken place during the war had entered into folklore. It had been told so many times and passed down from generation to generation that it was quite impossible to tell whether what I was hearing was a real account or something that had just become ingrained over five decades of storytelling. Naturally we only took statements from people who were alive at the time.

Scotland Yard had witnesses who claimed they had seen Serafinowicz execute Jews. We talked to people who confirmed there was no sign of him at the scene of the main massacre just outside Mir where more than a thousand Jews were murdered.

Serafinowicz was described by the Simon Wiesenthal Centre as the 'Commander' of the Belarussian police in Mir, but when you actually worked his rank out he was akin to a station sergeant. He was in command of about a dozen men. Before the outbreak of the war he'd have been busying his time working out who had stolen some chickens. He was in another village when the massacre occurred at Mir and nobody came forward to suggest otherwise, but he never tried to pretend to us that he hadn't known about it.

Like many people who had helped the Nazis, Serafinowicz only survived the war by switching sides and joining the Allies before it ended. By a complex route, he made his way to Britain via Italy, joining up to fight the Germans with a Balkan free regiment. Had he stayed in Belarus the Russians would have shot him as a German collaborator when they invaded.

He married a Polish woman in the UK and settled down to life as a carpenter in Surrey. By the time he came to see me in Hare Court, he understood perfectly well how the situation had caught up with him, but he was bitter about it because he saw himself as a net protector of local people. He insisted that more people would have died if he hadn't intervened with the Germans on behalf of the local population. He talked about going to villages where the Nazis wanted to shoot six men and convincing them only to shoot four. He said the Germans left it to the villagers to bring the four men forward, they didn't select them themselves. Sadly, it appears that the village idiots and the very elderly were the ones who ended up being shot.

I got the feeling Serafinowicz was not an enthusiastic anti-Semite, in fact he wasn't anti-Semitic at all. Like so many other people at that time in those circumstances, he was in a position where it was easier to conform than to rebel. Nobody, not even the witnesses who gave evidence for the prosecution at his committal, ever suggested he got any pleasure from killing people.

Serafinowicz ticked the CPS criteria because he was someone in a position of command, a decision-maker rather than a rank and file policeman. The reality is that if he had refused to help the Einsatzgruppen round up and dispose of local Jews he would probably have been shot himself. But once Scotland Yard had witnesses saying he had agreed to the Germans' demands, he was always going to be prosecuted.

Some of the prosecution evidence was pretty clear in supporting claims of Serafinowicz's participation in the killings. Some of its witnesses put him at the scene of the killings, pulling the trigger himself. He flatly denied this.

From my point of view the accounts of the prosecution witnesses dated back decades and their recollections of which policemen were present at killings were questionable. In the vast majority of cases their most recent written record of what they had seen had been created half a century afterwards. Some of the Jewish witnesses had made statements to the Simon Wiesenthal Centre, but even then those were given many years after the events in question.

Sixteen prosecution witnesses flew in for the committal hearing at Dorking Magistrates Court in April 1996, from as far afield as the US, South Africa, and Israel. Some were Jews who were now living elsewhere and others were non-Jews who had travelled over from Belarus.

I think the witnesses from Belarus found the whole experience bewildering. They were put up in a hotel and most of them had never seen plumbing before. They had to be taught about taps and toilets and flushing and things like that. They were all given witness expenses and a subsistence allowance, but I don't think they had been told to expect anything: one had brought chunks of dried meat to feed himself. They were very submissive to authority, which I suspect in Belarus has become ingrained over the years. If the Crown Prosecution Service told them to be in the lobby at 8am the following morning they would there on the dot of 8am.

The committal lasted 22 days because of the necessity for all the evidence to be interpreted, which slowed everything down, as did the need to pace the sessions to accommodate an 84-year-old defendant with a hearing problem.

His family turned up to support him but they weren't there every day. He was quite an independent man.

Although the committal wasn't a trial, it was my job to test what the witnesses claimed to have seen – Serafinowicz's involvement in the murder of a number of Jews in separate incidents. Some gave accounts of having seen events from a distance, or at night or from inside a building. None of them claimed to have been that close. I cross-examined all of them, gently. I never suggested they weren't telling the truth. I was merely probing.

The prosecution later dropped one of the four counts against Serafinowicz and the chief magistrate, Peter Badge, ruled there was no case to answer on another. But he decided there was a prima facie case to answer regarding the two remaining counts concerning the murders of three unnamed Jews in 1941. He ruled that a jury, properly directed, could reasonably conclude there was evidence to convict.

The case was committed to the Old Bailey where I would be crossing swords again with John Nutting, the man who had previously prosecuted in the Colin Stagg case. He was due to be led by Sir Derek Spencer QC, the Solicitor General. When a law officer prosecutes a case he always has a leading silk and at least two juniors behind him. Nutting had previously appeared for the prosecution at the committal proceedings.

Even before the trial was due to start in 1997, Serafinowicz's health was failing. By the time the case was due to be heard, he was extremely confused and his memory had gone. We instructed one of the country's leading experts in dementia who said that Serafinowicz was in no condition to stand trial and never would be.

The trial judge adjourned the case and ordered a 'fitness to plead' trial which would decide whether the trial would go ahead. At that hearing, some months later, the prosecution called a doctor who said that he thought Serafinowicz could follow the proceedings, and I called five who testified that he couldn't. Two of those psychiatrists had initially been employed by the prosecution. Throughout the 'fitness to plead' trial Serafinowicz didn't have a clue what was going on. He was just sitting in court dozing or dribbling. He was obviously very ill. He couldn't remember who I was from one day to the next, or why he was at the Old Bailey.

In January 1997, having been told in the very broadest of terms of the allegations against Serafinowicz, the jury decided very quickly that he wasn't fit to plead. That decision was vindicated seven months later when Serafinowicz died and a post mortem examination found that he was suffering from Alzheimer's Disease.

Nowadays a trial of the facts could have taken place without him being present, not to establish guilt, but to establish whether the acts at the centre of the case had taken place. The law has since changed and such 'fitness to plead' trials no longer take place.

I think Serafinowicz would have been an excellent

witness and I wouldn't have hesitated to call him. From a personal point of view the whole affair was quite frustrating because I didn't get to test the prosecution case before a jury. All our preparation for what would have been the first war crimes trial to involve Britain since the Nuremberg trials ended in 1947 had been in vain.

CHAPTER TEN

How to Become a QC

~

Becoming a Queen's Counsel is the pinnacle of achievement for a British barrister. A Queen's Counsel, or QC, is one of 'Her Majesty's Counsel learned in the law'. It's an honorific rank (King's Counsel, when there is a king on the English throne) which dates back to 1597 and is replete with the rich history, fancy costumes and occasional mumbo-jumbo of the English law.

It is also coveted, confers considerable status on its holders and can be highly lucrative.

In an intelligent and hard-working profession, Queen's Counsel are renowned for possessing especially sharp minds and smooth tongues. As a young junior barrister I viewed QCs as gods. They were set apart from me in garb and earnings. Whereas a barrister's gown is made of cotton, a QC's gown is of silk, hence the term 'taking silk', although in practice they are almost all artificial silk which is more hard wearing. Becoming a Queens Counsel can put barristers into a different league of earnings, for instance raising the fee received for a Legal Aid case by a third when compared to the fee paid to a junior barrister for doing the same case. But there can also be a downside: a new QC can price themselves out of some work. For example, a QC should not accept publicly-funded work unless a judge has granted permission for a silk to be instructed. In addition, some solicitors may think 'He's a very good junior but I'm not quite sure he's up to silk. I'd rather have a silk who's been doing it for a few years.' So, it is possible to end up getting less work and lose out. For some new silks who haven't been leading in cases before it can be a bit of a Catch 22 situation.

When a barrister believes they are ready to apply for silk they normally discuss the matter with their Head of Chambers and senior clerk. Luckily in 1990 my Head of Chambers, Michael Lewis, and my senior clerk, John Grimmer, were in favour. This was quite a turnaround from my early career. Then, becoming a QC seemed unobtainable because I had only just passed my law degree and ended up squatting in chambers.

However, once I had finally become a tenant at 3 Hare Court, I had observed the technique of all the lawyers I came across in court, whether alongside or in opposition, and I quickly felt that advocacy was something I could do as well as many of the silks I saw at close quarters.

Then, and now, it was not the done thing to tell your fellow tenants in chambers that you had applied for silk because you wouldn't want your colleagues to know that you had tried and failed. You might tell a couple of close friends, but you wouldn't broadcast the fact.

For a long time criminal practitioners were seen as operating at the dirty end of the profession and rather frowned upon, and not many were made up to silk. Whereas, say, if you were doing commercial law becoming a QC was thought to be much easier. As a result, so few silks specialised in criminal work that barristers who were expert in other fields suddenly turned up at the Old Bailey to do murder cases for the first time, with rather mixed results, just because the defendant required a QC. Nowadays criminal practitioners have become almost respectable and are recognised as specialists in their own right.

Taking silk is a curious procedure. When I applied over a quarter of a century ago being made a QC was entirely within the gift of the Lord Chancellor. It was a simple process. You merely applied on a sheet of paper, filled in how much money you had earned in the previous three years, put a stamp on the envelope and posted the letter.

The Lord Chancellor's Department asked senior judges, the leaders of the regional circuits (local groups of courts), the heads of the specialist bar associations (such as patents and family law) and others for their views on the applicants. Sometimes the request travelled further afield. The South Eastern Circuit, for instance, was so large that its leader could not know all of the candidates, so the list of applicants in the South East was also sent to all the chairs of the individual bar messes for Essex, Kent, Inner London and Middlesex. (A bar mess is a group of barristers who practise from a particular court or county. The Essex Bar Mess, for instance, represents the barristers who appear at Southend, Basildon and Chelmsford. The name stems from the fact that traditionally barristers ate lunch together).

Civil servants would consider the responses and draw up a list of successful applicants for the Lord Chancellor to approve.

Some candidates had natural advantages. Until the 1980s barristers who were also Members of Parliament were fast-tracked into silk. If you were from the same political party as the Lord Chancellor, becoming a QC was almost automatic. For the rest of us the process was susceptible to gossip, horsetrading and prejudice[4]. If the

4 Some horse-trading would go on. I was chairman of the Essex Bar Mess for three years and had to provide feedback on young barristers myself. If I had a candidate who worked in Essex that I felt really deserved silk and who was very good, I might meet up with the chairman of the Kent Bar Mess and buy him a drink before our meeting with the circuit leader. During our conversation I might ask 'Have you got anyone who's good in Kent who has applied?' and if he replied 'Yes I've got a really good woman' then I'd ask him to tell me about his candidate and he would enquire about mine. We would both end up putting in a word for our respective candidates. It was a good way of bolstering the claims for silk of decent barristers, but it was rather informal.

leader of a circuit or a senior judge were to say: 'This person must never get silk, they're not to be trusted', it would almost certainly be the kiss of death to a young barrister's hopes of becoming a QC. One liked to hope such feedback would only ever be given where appropriate, but one never knew.

In those days you received a letter informing you whether you had been successful a day before the names of the new QCs were announced which was always Maundy Thursday, the Thursday before Easter. I took silk in March 1991, in the middle of an armed robbery case at Chelmsford Crown Court. I had been up against the judge, Peter Beaumont QC (later the Recorder of London) several times when he was a prosecuting barrister and he made a little speech when he found out.

At the time only about 50 barristers obtained silk each year. My name was printed alongside the other triumphant candidates in the announcements in *The Times*. All the successful candidates were listed in order of seniority, with the barrister who had been a barrister the longest appearing first.

QCs have to take part in a ceremony in London which is among the finest pageants in the English social calendar. It lasts a full day and takes place in several stages, each with its own traditions and flummery.

For mine I hired the full historical costume of a silk from the outfitters Ede & Ravenscroft — buckled shoes, breeches, a frock coat, ruffs for your sleeves and a full-bottom wig. (Theoretically QCs may wear this get-up in court, but I don't know anyone who does. You would look a complete berk. Very few people buy the full-bottom wig after hiring one for the swearing-in ceremony because they cost thousands of pounds.)

I also wore a QC's gown, rather than my old barrister's gown. A barrister's gown is pleated with a fake pocket on the back, into which historically clients would place your fee, whereas a QC's gown is straight with no back pocket.

In the morning, I and my fellow QCs in-waiting were individually chauffeur-driven to the House of Lords, where the swearing-in took place in a room between the Lords and the Commons, next to a painting of the Battle of Waterloo. I swore an oath to the Queen before the Lord Chancellor, Lord Mackay of Clashfern.

My fellow 'Gang of Four' member Howard Godfrey was sworn in the same day, as was Patricia Scotland, later Baroness Scotland, who was the most junior barrister taking silk that year.

I took my parents Peter and Sheila, my then wife Wendy and my two children, Joanna and Peter, who were 15 and 12. Pride swelled up in my chest. It was a proud moment for my parents, and me. I think my father had given up hope of me becoming a pharmacist by then!

After being sworn in I received my QC's certificate (my 'letters patent') in a red envelope, before being driven back to chambers in my limousine. There followed a rushed lunch of sandwiches, washed down with some celebratory champagne before walking back to the Royal Courts of Justice, the gothic Victorian court complex just off the Strand, to attend the second ceremony of the day.

The morning 'swearing in' was very regimented but by the time we reached the 'bowing in' at the Lord Chief Justice's court at 2pm everyone was far more relaxed after the luncheon champagne.

Not surprisingly the court officials had a job trying to get everyone lined up again in order of seniority. Inside Court Four, the Lord Chief Justice turned to the senior silk in his court that day and formally requested a halt in proceedings, asking: 'Do you move?' The most senior new silk entered the room and bowed to the Lord Chief Justice, to the senior silk present in court, and finally to the junior bar sitting behind him.

After lunch it was usually quite impossible for all the new silks to bow in the right order and before you know where you were they were bowing in the wrong direction to the wrong person at the wrong time. It had all rather broken down by this stage, though nobody seemed to mind. After bowing in to the Lord Chief Justice the performance was repeated before the Master of the Rolls and the President of the Family Division. If you had a particular friend who happened to be a High Court judge, you might 'bow in' to his court, though that had to be arranged beforehand. Afterwards my family and I went back to chambers for a low-key drink and it was all over by 8pm. There were children present and I had to be back in court the following day, wearing a QC's robes.

When I took silk my earning power didn't alter that much straight away because I ended up doing exactly the same class of cases that I was doing before. For some time I been doing the same work as a QC, while getting around two-thirds of their fee.

However within a few years I began to land cases that I wouldn't have done had I not been a QC, such as Colin Stagg and Szymon Serafinowicz. It would have been inconceivable for the solicitors representing defendants in such big cases not to instruct a silk. These briefs paid well and enhanced my standing in the profession.

Nowadays the system for appointing silks is more formal. When Tony Blair's government modernised the profession in 2003, no silks were appointed for a few years while various reforms were considered. This didn't go down well with the legal profession, particularly with those who were hoping to apply for silk but also with judges. They liked having an upper tier of barristers because it gave them some control over what calibre of lawyer would appear in front of them. Eventually in 2005 the independent Queen's Counsel Selection Panel was established which consists of paid appointees who draw up a list for the Lord Chancellor to effectively rubber stamp.

Becoming a QC is more formal, complicated and expensive now. I paid nothing to apply and £50 for my letters patent. In 2017, an application costs several thousand pounds and, if successful, thousands of pounds more. Applicants who take the gamble must fill out a long and complicated form. The people who would previously have been asked what they thought about a candidate over a glass of sherry are landed with a mass of paperwork asking whether they are well versed in equality and diversity issues, how they have demonstrated that and so on.

Whether the new system actually comes up with different results is highly debatable, but it is undoubtedly fairer. At least now unsuccessful candidates get some feedback which helps them understand why they have been turned down, rather than wondering who has put a bad word in about them or why their face doesn't fit.

Today's swearing-in ceremonies take place at the more capacious Westminster Hall.

Successful candidates still arrive in chauffeur-driven limos and return to chambers for sandwiches and champagne before heading to the RCJ to 'bow in', but these days the Lord Chief Justice, Master of the Rolls and President of the Family Division sit in the same court room and are joined by the President of the Queen's Bench Division. The ceremony is the same but done in batches so all the family members can get into court to watch. The Lord Chief Justice now makes a speech which is very much directed at the new QCs' families.

If a member of my chambers is made a silk I always try to attend the 'bowing in' ceremony. If I'm not in court, I will go down to the Royal Courts of Justice and take a seat in the front row in Court Four so that I'm one of the senior silks they bow to. It's a prestigious moment for chambers when a tenant takes silk, and for the individual concerned it's often one of their most cherished days.

These days new QCs throw the most lavish parties to celebrate, hiring large hotel function rooms, the great halls at the Inns of Court and even the conservatory at the Barbican. They invite their families, friends, everyone from their chambers, solicitors and even judges to toast their good fortune. I have heard of people spending more than £20,000 on parties to celebrate taking silk. The best party I went to was probably thrown by Jim Sturman, my junior in the Colin Stagg case, which was attended by an extraordinary number of guests.

Sensible barristers always arrange such parties for a date when they are not in court the following day.

CHAPTER ELEVEN

Case 6
Andrusha the Bastard

~

It was -30C and my lips were so cold I could barely speak. I could see my breath turning into tiny droplets of ice before my eyes. The snow came up to my knees, chilling me to the bone and a biting wind whistled through the trees all around me. Wherever I had imagined my new career taking me as I celebrated passing my law exams in the 1970s, it certainly wasn't this desolate spot.

Once again, I had found myself in Belarus in the former Soviet Union, defending another former member of the wartime police accused of war crimes. Unlike his compatriot Szymon Serafinowicz, I found Anthony Sawoniuk a much more difficult man to represent. Sawoniuk had been known as 'Andrusha the bastard' by his fellow villagers in Domaczewo before he eagerly donned the Belarussian police uniform he was given by his Nazi paymasters. When the Germans invaded Belarus in 1941 Sawoniuk had already endured a very deprived childhood. The identity of his father was unknown – hence his rather unflattering soubriquet — and his mother struggled to provide for him from the meagre pay she earned taking in laundry for fellow villagers. Even by Belarussian standards the family was extremely poor.

The arrival of the Nazis had transformed Sawoniuk's fortunes and, tragically, those of the Jews. Prior to the outbreak of the Second World War the Jewish and Gentile populations in Belarus had apparently rubbed along pretty well. Sawoniuk himself showed no evidence of anti-Semitism before the war.

However, he was given the opportunity to join the police force by the invading Germans, who desperately needed to recruit more officers to maintain order and release German soldiers for the Eastern front. It was the only job available to Sawoniuk because, unlike the other villagers, he and his mother didn't own any land on which they could scratch a living. Nonetheless, he was said to have joined the Belarussian police enthusiastically and, when the orders came to exterminate the Jews he played an active role in hunting down those Jews who had survived the 'Final Solution' mass killings taking place in settlements across the country.

Like Serafinowicz, Sawoniuk had made himself scarce before the Russians liberated Belarus and ended up fighting on the side of the Allies at the end of the war, although it later emerged he had served with a Waffen-SS unit prior to that. He came to Britain via a similar route to Serafinowicz after fighting with the Free Italian Army and ended up living in Bermondsey, south London, working on the railways.

Again, like Serafinowicz, the Simon Wiesenthal Centre had publicised the evidence against Sawoniuk. After Serafinowicz's trial collapsed, Scotland Yard and the Crown Prosecution Service realised that unless they relaxed their prosecution criteria anyone they could charge with war crimes was likely to be too elderly or infirm to face trial.

By then anybody in a position of command during the early 1940s would have been in their late 80s or early 90s, but Sawoniuk was still a teenager at the time his crimes allegedly took place. At the time of his arrest he was in his late 70s and in rude health. He was deemed to be physically able to survive the court process and came within the grasp of the prosecuting authorities.

After Sawoniuk's arrest in September 1997 I was the obvious candidate to represent him because I was the only barrister in Britain who had led the defence in a war crimes trial. So it was back to Belarus again, but this time in slightly different circumstances.

The same officers from the Scotland Yard unit who had gone out to Mir, along with the same CPS solicitors this time went to Domaczewo to gather evidence for the prosecution and it was all disclosed to us just as it had been in the Serafinowicz case. Once again John Nutting had been appointed to prosecute the case, leading John Kelsey-Fry, another formidable opponent.

Sawoniuk's village was further south than Mir so when we went to Belarus to gather our own evidence we based ourselves in Brest-Litovsk. There was a dearth of witnesses willing to say anything positive about Sawoniuk. It appeared that after being accepted into the police he had become a rather officious, bossy and unpopular person in his village. He appeared to be the classic example of someone who had been bullied all his life making the most of an unexpected chance to get his own back.

The Germans had given him some purpose in his life when he hadn't had any before. Now he had a regular income and a gun. He could boss a few people about and feel good about himself, whereas before he had been bullied by his peers as a child because he didn't have a father.

We had evidence that Serafinowicz had gone out on a limb to save some lives at least, but we didn't have that with Sawoniuk. He was charged with four specimen counts of murdering Jews in 1942 in separate incidents which took place during the 'mopping up' operation to eliminate those who had not been massacred by the Nazis' Einsatzgruppen regiments.

Like Serafinowicz, Sawoniuk was on Legal Aid but I had no problem with that. He had paid taxes in Britain for more than 50 years and was entitled to a fair trial. When I represented him and Serafinowicz, both had lived here for longer than I had been alive.

When I met Sawoniuk I found him to be quite aggressive. He was angry at his predicament, which he felt was deeply unfair. He appeared to have no insight into the position the Jews had in his country and to have embraced the Nazi philosophy wholeheartedly. He was aggrieved. He had a strong Russian accent and would shout at me in conference.

I didn't find him an easy man to like, though that wasn't important. Like all lawyers I have represented a lot of people I didn't like over the years, people who have done the most horrendous things. But it's surprising how many people you represent where you can see something positive about them even when the charges are quite serious. Serafinowicz fitted into that category, Sawoniuk less so.

There were more victims and more witnesses against 'Andrusha the Bastard' than in the case of Serafinowicz. For one charge Sawoniuk was accused of shooting a number of Jews in an atrocity that another villager claimed to have witnessed, albeit from a distance. Again we visited Belarus to gather evidence and I decided we should visit the scene. Which was how I came to be standing knee deep in the snow wondering about the strange turn that my career had taken. The Belarus winter was hard and long.

Nonetheless, it was only by visiting the forest to check the location of an incident where Sawoniuk was said to have shot three Jewish women and where the witness was that I formed the view that it was impossible to identify anybody at that distance. The witness might have been able to see someone in a police uniform and get an idea of their build, but to actually say for sure it was Sawoniuk as opposed to any other policeman? I just felt the distance was too great. The witness had been at the top of a hill in an area of scrub. We knew where they were pretty accurately because they had described it quite carefully, and we knew where the shooting was alleged to have taken place. It was simply a question of being able to judge the distance for ourselves.

When we got back to England another month-long committal took place, this time at Bow Street Magistrates Court in London, in April 1998. Once again a host of witnesses were flown over from Belarus for the hearing, at the end of which the magistrate presiding ruled that Sawoniuk did have a case to answer. He sent him to trial charged with four counts of murder between 19 September – 31 December 1942, two of Jewish men and two of Jewish women. All counts were specimen charges for incidents involving the deaths of a larger number of Jews.

At one of the preliminary hearings at the Old Bailey, my bluff was well and truly called. I indicated I was going to apply to stay one of the charges against Sawoniuk, where the witness claimed to see Sawoniuk shooting from the hill, on the grounds that my client couldn't possibly have a fair trial unless the jury were able to see the location for themselves. To the surprise of everyone present, the judge announced: 'Well why can't we go and have a look?' I had been trumped. As a result, the jury, judge, legal teams and all the court officials, accompanied by an army of reporters, travelled out to Belarus for a week in the middle of the prosecution case at the Old Bailey, in March 1999, so that they could see the place where the shooting allegedly happened and many other sites which featured in the trial. It was a unique event which must have cost tens of thousands of pounds.

Everyone stayed in the same hotel in Brest including the jurors, the court officials and the media. It was the only hotel big enough to accommodate everyone. The jury were confined to certain parts of the hotel and a dining area from which the media and lawyers were barred. In turn jurors were told not to go to other areas of the hotel. Out of sympathy for the media that included the bar. Ushers policed the divide, though no one tried to break the rules.

It was quite a media event. All the newspapers and major broadcasters sent at least one or two journalists. We usually met them in the bar every evening to drink beer and vodka. Fortunately, the reporters made it quite clear that when we were together it was Chatham House rules, and that therefore everything said between ourselves was 'off the record' and not for publication. They were as good as their word.

Every night they would discuss how they could report what had happened earlier in the day. The trial judge, Mr Justice Potts, wore a red bobble hat throughout the jury visit because it was bitterly cold and there was some discussion about what it could be called. Someone described it as being like Noddy's hat and I remember Don Mackay of *The Mirror* saying: 'You can't say the judge was wearing a Noddy hat, he'll have you up for contempt!' Eventually it was decided that would be an inappropriate way to describe the judge's headwear.

The jury was taken to Domaczewo to see where Sawoniuk and the witnesses lived and the location of the police station, the ghetto, and the hill where the witness claimed to have seen Sawoniuk shooting a victim, which led to us all being there in the first place. When we climbed the hill the forest was deep in snow. But the visit was certainly beneficial to the jury because it would have been nigh on impossible to imagine the scene without physically being there. Once again we had an interpreter with us. The Belarussians largely left us alone by now, having grown more accustomed to us.

When everyone else went back to England after the jury visit myself and the lawyers from both sides took advantage of the few days' adjournment ordered by the judge to stay on and take video evidence from an old lady who had been unable to get to us during our earlier trip. She lived in the middle of nowhere and we had to drag the camera and tripod across fields deep in snow to get to her house. It was almost dark by the time we made it. We filmed her evidence, which we regarded as useful background, in her one and only room. At one point her cat was caught on camera as it disappeared up the chimney. The only question the jury asked after her evidence was played to the court later in the trial was 'What happened to the cat?'

The prosecution case was compelling. One of the major problems we faced was that most witnesses did not appear to have any ulterior motive for naming Sawoniuk as the murderer. Multiple witnesses named him in circumstances which tended to indicate a pattern of behaviour that supported the Crown's case. Crucially — and unfairly I thought — the jury heard evidence suggesting Sawoniuk had been involved in the killing of other Jews outside the four counts he faced. My objections to these going before the court failed. The powerful testimony of the prosecution witnesses who travelled from Belarus must have weighed on the jury's minds. There was also an expert, a Professor Browning from Canada, who gave evidence about the background of what had happened during the war and the 'Final Solution'. It really painted a picture for the jury and was always going to be difficult to counter.

Nevertheless, at the end of the prosecution case, at 'half-time', I made a 'no case' submission to the trial judge, Mr Justice Potts. It proved successful in part, because he threw out two of the four specimen charges against Sawoniuk — the murders of the two Jewish men — on the grounds of insufficient evidence. Of the remaining two counts, one was based on the testimony of a boy who was only 13 at the time when he claimed to have seen 'Andrusha' shoot 15 Jews, and the other was the incident witnessed from the top of the hill that led to the murder of three more Jews. I was surprised that count survived my submission.

I had not intended calling Sawoniuk as a witness — but he insisted on giving evidence against my advice. My heart sank. As a barrister I can do my best to warn a defendant about the pitfalls of entering the witness box, but in the end the decision is theirs. Sawoniuk was determined to give evidence, despite me asking him to consider whether doing so would improve his chances of a not guilty verdict. I felt he would only make things worse.

Sawoniuk was the only witness I called for the defence. While he had been in the dock I had been able to keep him under a degree of control, but once he entered the witness box I was prevented by convention from speaking to him until he had finished his evidence. I had run the case on the basis that nobody could be sure after all this time that the identification evidence was reliable, that it was a very long time ago to remember, and that mistakes could easily have been made. Sawoniuk claimed the prosecution witnesses had made it all up and that he was the victim of a conspiracy. It didn't help that he told the court that he had left Domaczewo in 1943, when I had conducted the case in accordance with his instructions, namely that he had left much later.

My advice to Sawoniuk had been not to argue with John Nutting, prosecution counsel, and to listen carefully to what he asked and to answer succinctly. I also urged him not to wander off topic. Sawoniuk ignored all of this.

The courtroom saw a clash of styles. Nutting was very courteous to Sawoniuk. In return Sawoniuk was argumentative and aggressive. He came across as cantankerous, ignorant and stubborn. Over two days, Nutting reeled him in, slowly, surely. Devastatingly.

There is no way of knowing what the verdict would have been had Sawoniuk not given evidence. It might have been just the same, but I felt his chances would have been better had he not entered the witness box. The jury were out overnight, but I wasn't surprised when they returned with guilty verdicts the following morning. Sawoniuk was sentenced to life imprisonment. He was still protesting his innocence as he left the dock for prison. He cut a pathetic figure as he was led away. It was the first and only successful prosecution in Britain for war crimes committed during the Second World War.

I gave notice of appeal, on the grounds that the evidence for the two guilty counts was too scant to go before the jury. I also complained that the jury should not have heard evidence about Sawoniuk's other alleged killings outside of the charges. In 2000, the Lord Chief Justice, Lord Bingham, upheld the original verdict. Sawoniuk remained in Norwich Prison where he died in 2005. Of all the war criminals who committed atrocities during the Second World War he didn't strike me as an important or significant individual — Andrusha the Bastard, aged 17 when war broke out, later becoming a police constable.

I always believed that the War Crimes Act was 'too

little too late' and that the resulting prosecutions were an undistinguished episode in British justice. Putting Sawoniuk on trial a decade after the end of the Second World War would have been perfectly acceptable, but to wait five decades, when he had been living openly in Britain all that time? It wasn't a case of someone who had only just been found, as was the case with some of the Nazis extradited from South America.

Even though neither went particularly well for me, the Serafinowicz and Sawoniuk cases fascinated me professionally. In 2012, my wife Gay and I visited the Museum of Terror in Berlin, where a display catalogued the war crimes trials after the Allied victory. Both Serafinowicz and Sawoniuk were featured, along with my name. I wasn't quite sure how to feel in the circumstances.

CHAPTER TWELVE

Defending Fraudsters

~

Another specialism that I developed was the defence of those accused of serious and complex fraud. Although fraud is less dramatic and consequently attracts less publicity than my other more violent fields, I find it fascinating nonetheless. While murder cases come with conflicting witness evidence and reams of paperwork, they are not difficult to understand. Fraud cases are usually more of an intellectual challenge, mostly in working out how a market or industry operates.

In my first really big case, I defended Wallace Duncan Smith, a banker in the City of London, who was accused of carrying out fraudulent trades. I was engaged by his solicitor, Matthew Frankland, with whom I have developed a lasting business relationship and friendship. Mr Smith's was my first large fraud trial and the first Serious

Fraud Office prosecution in which I appeared as a silk.

The main challenge for me was understanding the case. The Wallace Smith Trust Corporation was a failing merchant bank that had gone bust. Mr Smith, the managing director, who was 59, stood accused of siphoning money out of the bank to a series of Canadian trusts, which in turn made 'capital injections' of roughly £1m-a-year back into the bank. As the bank's losses worsened, Mr Smith resorted to further chicanery to convince his clients, fellow directors, auditors and the Bank of England that it was healthy, paying more than £50m for fictitious Canadian government bonds. He also allegedly engaged in 'double dipping': pledging certificates of deposit twice over to different parties.

Eventually his fellow directors became suspicious and he was forced to come clean. In April 1991 he called in the Bank of England and the whole house of cards came tumbling down. The Wallace Smith Trust Corporation ceased trading and was wound up. Around 140 people lost their jobs and financial institutions in London were left with debts of £90 million. Not long afterwards the Bank of England called in the City of London Police and the Serious Fraud Office.

Mr Smith's trial took place in 1993 at Chichester Rents, a special fraud court in London's Chancery Lane which had rooms large enough to cope with all the documentation required for massive fraud cases. In 1996 the Maxwell brothers, Ian and Kevin, were tried and acquitted there of defrauding pension funds overseen by their crooked father, Robert Maxwell, the newspaper tycoon. Chichester Rents had no fixed furniture so that benches, tables or chairs could be moved around to accommodate the voluminous paperwork. There was no dock and the defendant sat with his lawyers.

Despite still being based on a mass of paper and testimony delivered in person, Mr Smith's trial took a step into modernity. For the first time an English court took live video link evidence from abroad. Our sitting hours were adapted to allow satellites to beam video pictures live from other time zones: we sat at 7.30am on some days to hear from witnesses in Australia and the Far East and late on others for evidence from Canada.

During his three-month trial, Mr Smith denied any wrongdoing whatsoever. His defence was that all the transactions were genuine. I envisaged little prospect of an acquittal, but I had to do my very best for him and test the prosecution case. Personally, I found him very affable. He had quite a pronounced Canadian accent and was quietly spoken and enormously polite. He hadn't been making any money out of the fraud at all, save for his income, which wasn't especially extravagant. He was just keeping the bank afloat by exaggerating its liquidity. He seemed to have got away with it once and just carried on, until things spiralled out of control. I suspected his main motivation was pride. He didn't actually live a particularly flamboyant lifestyle. He had a country house in Hampshire and a flat in the City, both of which had been purchased long before anything started going wrong. I think he liked the fact he was chairman of a merchant bank and could not face the ignominy of it going bust.

Mr Smith chose of his own volition not to give evidence, which was wise in my opinion because I'm not sure he would have been a good witness. He was intelligent and erudite, but I could see him tying himself up in knots trying to explain away the deals he did with his Canadian counterparties who, in truth, did not exist.

He was acquitted of three of seven counts and the judge directed a verdict of not guilty on a fourth. He was convicted of fraudulent trading and two counts of obtaining property by deception involving sums of £26m and £11m. He didn't show much emotion at the verdict. The trial judge, Mr Justice Tuckey, said it was no mitigation that only banks and big institutions had lost money. He stated that Smith's actions had damaged the reputation of the City of London and jailed him for six years.

We took his case to appeal in 1995 but lost. The Criminal Cases Review Commission later referred the case back to the Court of Appeal and there were further appeals, but they, too, were unsuccessful. I didn't represent him in those.

If I thought the amount of paperwork involved in the Wallace Smith Trust Corporation trial was immense it was nothing compared to my next big fraud case. Butte Mountain in Montana in the United States was once known as 'the richest hill on Earth' and had been mined for its incredible reserves of gold, silver and zinc since the 19th Century 'gold rush'. It had yielded more gold than any other mountain in the world.

When the price of gold was fixed at $35-an-ounce in the 1970s, however, it became too costly to extract the gold and its American owners ceased operations. Most of the gold had been taken out but, as with all mines, some had been left in the ground because its value was below the cost of extraction.

Everyone agreed that a great deal of gold had been left in Butte Mountain and when the gold price shot up astronomically in the 1980s, those reserves became attractive to mine again. Advances had also been made in underground mining which enabled much gold to be extracted by machines, rather than by men with pickaxes.

A British firm, Butte Mining, had purchased the mine from its previous American owners and had carried out tests to ascertain how much gold was left and whether it was worth taking out. Butte Mining concluded that the mountain had a viable future.

So it came to pass that Butte Mining floated on the London Stock Exchange, selling shares to investors in return for money to exploit the mine. This was followed by a rights issue where more money was raised from shareholders to finish the project. Investors thought they were taking part in a second 'Gold Rush', but as time wore on they became suspicious. Butte Mining Plc eventually went bust, wiping out the holdings of investors, most of whom were British. The London Stock Exchange called in the Serious Fraud Office.

The allegation was that the company had misled investors about the mine's reserves and its economic viability. Butte Mining's British chairman, financier, another high-ranking official, and a mining expert were all prosecuted on conspiracy charges. I was engaged to represent the company's mining expert, a 40-year-old Welshman called Kenneth Clews, who had estimated the mountain's remaining gold and the cost of extracting it.

Defending him at the trial, which took place at Chichester Rents between June 1997 and May 1998, was a vast and time-consuming endeavour. I, my two junior barristers Brian Altman and Alison Popal, and a solicitor, James Carlton, put in extraordinary hours trying to understand the case. All week we would meet for tea at 7am and finish at 8pm. These were long and demanding days, especially when towards the end of the trial I was preparing for the committal in the Anthony Sawoniuk case and for the trial of a solicitor accused of a mortgage fraud. (When I am working on a long trial I have always found switching between cases easy because each comes as light relief to the other.)

Our room adjoining the court was stuffed full of plans, diagrams, tunnel charts dating back to the 19th Century. James Carlton flew to Butte to gather evidence. He reported that it was a ghastly place: all the detritus from the washing of the gold had been dumped in a small lake dating back to the glory days of the original 'gold rush'. To this day the lake is said to be so poisonous that any bird that lands in it dies.

When instructed in a fraud trial I often try and have an expert working alongside me to brief me and my team on the relevant industry, whether it's the derivatives market, LIBOR, or floating a company on the Stock Exchange. Unless you understand how the system works you can't understand what has gone wrong. For the Butte trial, we engaged the services of Tim Shaw, emeritus professor of mining engineering at the Royal School of Mines, Imperial College, London. Professor Shaw was invaluable and helped me understand all the documentation and explain the mining processes and the difficulty of getting to various parts of the mine to extract the gold.

Mr Clews' trial turned on whether he honestly believed the amount of gold and the cost of extracting it, as declared by the company, was an accurate statement or whether it was exaggerated. In essence, the prosecution alleged that he and the money men knew the mountain wasn't economically viable and that the whole flotation amounted to a giant swindle.

Mr Clews had studied the mine prior to lending his support to Butte Mining Plc's plans. As well as thousands of old maps detailing the layout of the mine and its miles of tunnels, he had access to tens of thousands of rock samples dating back to when the mine was previously in production showing the percentage of gold contained in the rock accessed by various tunnels underground.

He insisted that all his professional knowledge led him to believe that the facts outlined in the prospectus issued to investors were true. He was a mining expert, he said, and wasn't involved in the financial side of the flotation; it was his three co-defendants who were the professional businessmen.

Detail poured into every nook and cranny of the case. The Crown called something like 15 to 20 experts on every aspect of mining that you could imagine, all of whom had to be cross-examined to support our contention that Butte mountain really was worth mining. The Crown's experts chiefly said that the gold inside Butte mountain was going to be too difficult to find and extract. Its mining specialists said the machines purchased by Butte Mining couldn't get down certain tunnels to reach some of the reserves, while its hydrologists claimed that the extraction of other deposits would cause water to enter the mine. Professor Shaw said that by the time the case had finished I could probably have obtained an undergraduate degree in mining.

The case had its moments. One mining expert we consulted came to a conference in my chambers on a rather cold day back when we didn't have any central heating at 3 Hare Court. He was an elderly gentleman and he kept his coat on throughout the conference. When we stopped for a break I think he'd treated himself to a pretty good lunch, because when we reconvened in the afternoon, he seemed to be drowsy and to be having difficulty following the discussions. We had a little gas fire in the centre of the room and he had commandeered the warmest spot next to it, which sadly didn't assist him in his efforts to stay awake, but he certainly woke up when his coat caught fire. A rather pungent and unpleasant smell emanated from his smouldering coat. We had to pat him down.

My client Mr Clews was the only one of the four defendants found not guilty of any wrongdoing regarding the flotation of the company: the jury felt that it couldn't be proved beyond reasonable doubt that he knew what he was saying about the gold was untrue. Unfortunately, he was convicted of conspiracy to defraud shareholders by overstating the mine's potential for the rights issue. He was sentenced to 18 months in prison, less than any of his co-defendants.

Despite lasting almost a year the trial never became tedious. We were working too hard for that to happen. But during such a long trial there is a danger one can become too consumed by a case. It almost becomes your life.

The Butte Mining case was one of the last to be heard at Chichester Rents. The set-up was felt to be too expensive for a criminal tribunal and the authorities decided not to renew the lease when it eventually ran out. The Rents were very user friendly, but rumour has it that I contributed to their decline. Apparently, the weight of the paperwork in the Butte Mining case exceeded the weight load of the floor.

CHAPTER THIRTEEN

Case 7
Convicted by Earprint

~

As my career has developed, so has forensic science. In particular DNA profiling has allowed the police to identify many criminals from trace evidence such as blood and hair left at a crime scene. However, it is important that courts do not place too much weight on scientific techniques which are still open to doubt.

Many criminals are caught because they leave behind their fingerprints. Experts dust crime scenes for fingertip marks and match their contours to suspects to identify who has left the print. Fingerprinting has a wholly respectable pedigree dating back decades. Sadly, the same cannot be said for earprints. In fact, until the murder of a pensioner in 1996 there had been, to my knowledge, only one other time they had been used in English courts. When I was called to inspect the files in 2001, I believed that the conviction of a young man for the murder of Dorothy Wood, a 94-year-old former health visitor, was unsafe. The details of the case were extraordinary.

Because she had difficulty walking, Mrs Wood, who was arthritic and deaf, slept downstairs in her house in Huddersfield, West Yorkshire. One night in May 1996 an intruder used a jemmy or a screwdriver to force open a transom window above her bed. The intruder climbed through the window and smothered Mrs Wood with a pillow. When the police examined her house they found an earprint on the outside of a downstairs window. The window had been cleaned recently and was otherwise unmarked.

With no other leads to pursue, the police took earprints from several local burglars and called in the services of a Dutch policeman, Cornelis van der Lugt. Although he had no formal forensic science qualifications, Mr van der Lugt had studied earprints in great detail and believed them to be as unique to an individual as fingerprints. He told detectives that the print left on the window pane was identical to the sample print taken from one of the burglars, Mark Dallagher. Mr Dallagher, who had gained access to properties through transom windows in the past, was charged with Mrs Wood's murder. The theory was that he had pressed his ear against the glass to see if he could hear whether anyone was at home.

At Mr Dallagher's trial at Leeds Crown Court in 1998, Mr van der Lugt appeared as an expert witness for the prosecution. He told the jury he was 'absolutely convinced' that the earprint found on the window belonged to Mr Dallagher. His evidence was supported in part by a pathologist, Professor Peter Vanezis, who said it was highly likely the print was Mr Dallagher's, although he admitted that he couldn't be 100% sure. Unfortunately, this being an area of forensic science hitherto almost unknown to the English criminal law, no ear expert could be found for the defence to contradict the prosecution's claim. The trial judge allowed the jury to hear about Mr Dallagher's previous burglaries. Aged 22, Mr Dallagher, who maintained his innocence, was convicted of murder and jailed for life.

For an appeal Mr Dallagher's new solicitor, Simon Mackay, and my junior, Jim Sturman, managed to gather evidence from other experts who had spent many hours looking at people's ears and who maintained that it was impossible to positively identify anybody by analysing an earprint alone. They were a Professor Moenssens from the US, a Professor van Koppen from the Netherlands and a Dr Champod from the Forensic Science Service in Solihull. Their view was that, at best, studying an earprint only allowed you to rule out a suspect. For example, if one suspect had a particularly long ear lobe and another didn't, you could probably exclude one as the owner of a particular earprint, but you couldn't actually confirm it had been left by the other. The experts cast considerable doubt on the reliability of the prosecution's science.

Normally judges leave defence counsel to conduct their case how they see fit, so there was no duty on the part of the original trial judge to intervene when van der Lugt's evidence wasn't contradicted at the original trial. For all the judge knew the defence had commissioned an expert who had agreed with the prosecution ear expert. (Defence lawyers don't have to call unhelpful witnesses.) As it happened, the defence team had made considerable efforts to find experts in earprint evidence to no avail. There was no question of those defending Mr Dallagher being negligent.

Nonetheless, the outcome of the case was questionable: if you removed the earprint evidence from the prosecution, there was simply no case. When I met Mr Dallagher, it was clear he wasn't the brightest of men, but he had a burning sense of injustice, as you might expect. He once told me: 'I might do a bit of burglary but I don't go around murdering old ladies'.

The Criminal Cases Review Commission [set up after the string of miscarriages of justice mentioned in *Chapter Seven: Helen Hodgson*] referred the case back to the Court of Appeal in 2002. The new defence experts all gave evidence to the appeal hearing, which I led at the Court of Appeal on 4-5 July 2002.

By this time, a BBC documentary unit, *Rough Justice*, was championing Mr Dallagher's case. The *Rough Justice* team got quite excited and turned up at my home in

Suffolk to film me preparing for the case sitting in front of a large pile of papers, reading them, and turning page after page, then getting up to have my cornflakes before jumping into my car and driving to London. I think it was all done to humanise the role of a barrister. I assume they wanted to try and show that the defendant was being represented by a real person.

The essence of my case was that the new earprint evidence, unavailable to the defence at trial, made the verdict unsafe. As is usual at appeal, I made several arguments in 'the alternative'. That is, I tried a belt and brace approach employing competing arguments. When arguing in the alternative, lawyers argue for Proposition A, but add that if the judges or jury find that Proposition A is wrong, then they should consider Proposition B.

I laid before the court four grounds for why the conviction should be quashed. The first was that the prosecution's earprint evidence was so unreliable it was inadmissible. The second was that even if it was admissible, the new defence earprint evidence would have allowed a more thorough cross-examination of Mr van der Lugt and Professor Vanezis using the points made by those defence experts. Thirdly, in the absence of the defence experts, the prosecutors were able to present their case using the 'prosecutor's fallacy' — that is to overstate the probability of a defendant being guilty. Fourthly, I argued that the trial judge was wrong to allow the jury to hear about Mr Dallagher's criminal record.

The appeal court judges, all very experienced, looked at each ground in turn. Firstly, on the strength of the earprint evidence, they noted Mr van der Lugt's 27 years as a police officer in Holland and that he had lectured at the Dutch Police College, but also that he had no formal qualifications. They recorded:

> He had simply become interested in earprint identification and read what was available on the topic. He had built up a portfolio of about 600 photographs and 300 earprints and from his experience and from what he had read he was satisfied that no two earprints are alike in every particular.

By contrast, Dr Champod, the defence expert, noted that in Switzerland earprints left at the scene were compared with controlled prints to assist in the early stages of the investigation, adding: 'But on occasions those believed to have left earprints have been found to have genuine alibis.' He pointed out that neither the Forensic Science Service in the UK nor the FBI in the US compared earprints.

The appeal court judges ruled that even without the new expert evidence now relied upon by the defence the trial judge was right to have allowed the earprint science to be placed before the jury. They ruled it was admissible.

But, crucially, when it came to the second of my grounds, they agreed that the fresh expert evidence might have caused the jury to return a different verdict. The judges said it 'might reasonably have affected the approach of the trial jury to the crucial identification evidence of the experts and thus have affected the decision of the jury to convict.'

They did not need to make a finding on the third and fourth grounds. Mr Dallagher's conviction was quashed and a re-trial ordered.

Shortly before the start of the re-trial in 2004, which Jim Sturman, now a QC, led for the defence, the prosecution revealed that they had subjected the original earprint to new mitochondrial DNA techniques and were awaiting the results.

Ten days into the proceedings the results of the tests were dramatically disclosed to the defence, and confirmed that whoever the DNA from the earprint belonged to it wasn't Mr Dallagher — he could be eliminated as its source.

The trial was abandoned to allow the prosecution team to further review the case and Mr Dallagher was freed on bail. At a further hearing at the Old Bailey in 2004, the Crown Prosecution Service offered no evidence and he was formally found not guilty.

The documentary team filmed him at home following his release. Sadly he had become institutionalised. He was sleeping in a separate room from his partner in a single bed which he made every day just as he would have had he still been in prison or in the army, folding everything up in a military way. He called his bedroom a 'cell'.

Lawyers had helped right a wrong. Credit was due to Simon Mackay and Jim Sturman, who had dug up the extra experts. But the BBC's journalists had helped, too. If something needed funding, *Rough Justice* would make the money available.

No legal system is perfect and any system with human beings making the decisions is bound to result in the occasional error. The sooner those errors can be corrected the better and I believe it is vital that our justice system is scrutinised in this way.

CHAPTER FOURTEEN

Winning the Trust of a Judge

~

When I was a young barrister a judge called Gerald Thesiger used to scare the living daylights out of me. He had a fearsome reputation which preceded him by some distance, and I vividly remember that trepidation flowed through my veins as I prepared to address him for the first time at the Old Bailey. When the time came I looked up at his face — and it felt like he was looking so far down his nose at me that he could hardly see me at all. For all I know he might have been a perfectly pleasant individual in private, but that certainly wasn't the image he wanted to convey in court.

To the average man or woman in the street, the average judge probably looks like Mr Justice Thesiger — male, the wrong side of 60, austere, shrouded in his own self-importance, detached, unapproachable and irascible.

But while that stereotype was probably largely correct 50 years ago, in my experience the fearsome bewigged, grey-haired hawk peering distastefully down at the assembled barristers, defendants and jurors below, itching to lock up someone for life, is a creature of the past.

Judges are much more sympathetic and in touch with ordinary people than most would think. They normally travel on public transport and they have the same worries over money and mortgages and children as the rest of us. Surprising though it might seem, they share the same human qualities and frailties, too.

I know this because I am a judge myself. When I am not representing clients, I sit part-time at the Old Bailey trying criminal cases. Britain is, I believe, unique in Europe in appointing part-time judges, called recorders[5], to sit in criminal, civil and family cases. The rest of the time we work as barristers, solicitors or academics. So a barrister may appear as an advocate on Friday in one court and on Monday be sitting as a part-time judge in another.

Like many other aspects of the law, the judiciary has its own traditions and quirks. When I first sat at the Old Bailey all judges were still given small bunches of flowers called nosegays four times a year at the start of each legal term, because the court was originally built over Newgate Prison and in those days the judges would carry nosegays

---

5 *Originally a part-time judge, called a recorder, was appointed by the corporation of a city or town to 'record' the proceedings in their court, hence the name.*

to help ward off the stench from the cells below. Although the flowers are now only given out once a year, the practice continues.

Another tradition at the Old Bailey is that the court presided over by the most senior judge displays one of the five great swords of the City of London. If the senior judge adjourns the sword is placed in the court of the next most senior judge. One day early in my judicial career I was sitting later than normal and was the only judge left when to my surprise the court door opened and an attendant sombrely carried in the sword and laid it on the bench. I think the defendant thought I might be proposing a rapid beheading.

Sitting as a recorder has enriched my understanding of the law. I applied to become one in 1987, because I was thinking of applying for silk, and the feeling was at the time that being a recorder would help. Whether that was the case I now very much doubt but I have come to value the time that I sit as a judge and recognise the importance of the job and the contribution it makes.

I can try every type of criminal case except terrorism, murder, manslaughter and a few rare offences such as a breach of the Official Secrets Act. Traditionally crown court judges have not specialised, but nowadays special training must be undertaken for some offences. Judges aren't allowed to try rape cases, for example, unless they've got what is rather unfortunately called a 'sex ticket', which means they've been on special courses to educate them about the issues around that offence. The system was introduced to try to ensure judges don't make the kind of ghastly gaffe which made the newspapers too often in the past.

The best judges have the ability to distill a complicated case in a way that a jury can understand. When appearing as a barrister in a big case I will have a junior or two and a team of solicitors helping me and often an expert to advise, and the prosecutor will have the same degree of support, but the judge has just himself. The ability to absorb so much information, understand all the nuances and sum up a trial succinctly and simply is an art. When you've had to do it yourself, you soon realise how well some judges do it (and also how badly it can be done on occasion.)

A good summing-up should be absolutely neutral. The best tribute I can pay a judge after all the evidence has been heard and the summing-up has been delivered is to say to myself: 'Well, whatever happens now I can't complain about the judge, we have had a fair trial.'

Judges tend to improve with age. When I was called to the bar a few judges sat into their 80s. Now judges retire at 70, which I find slightly ridiculous. Just as everyone is living longer and staying more active later in life — and as other people work longer — judges must retire when they are younger. A number of extremely good judges who could carry on are being lost. Many wish there was some sort of MoT certificate that would allow them to sit for a few more years. Peter Beaumont, the recently retired Recorder of London, who was an excellent judge, could easily have continued and now sits part-time in the Channel Islands where the enforced retirement age does not apply.

Of the hundreds of judges I have appeared in front of during my career, the most impressive was Lord Bingham, the former Lord Chief Justice. He was a man of formidable and astonishing intelligence. I think most barristers would agree he was one of the greatest judges of all time, certainly since the Second World War. He had legendary status as an appellant judge, and I appeared in front of him in the Court of Appeal and the Privy Council. His mastery of the facts and his knowledge and ability to apply the law were awesome. He was also very courteous. Lawyers who had prepared their cases properly weren't intimidated by the thought of appearing in front of him, but if you hadn't done your homework, you would be exposed.

As a barrister, I've always thought it's desirable to be well-prepared and on good terms with a judge, because you tend to get what you want more often, whereas an ill-prepared or rude advocate is less likely to be successful. I don't think any judge would consciously take against an advocate, but subconsciously if they think someone has been talking rubbish for weeks they may be less inclined to listen to them when they say something that does make sense. If a jury see you arguing with the judge all the time it may well cause them to doubt your reliability. Likewise, if you appear too familiar with the judge; you've got to pitch your approach just right.

When I began my career judges often adopted a Patrician attitude towards juries, some markedly so. Modern judges try to make themselves as approachable and user-friendly as possible. Juries are more relaxed if they think that the court is being presided over by a normal human being who is on their side.

Judges are very conscious of a jury's time. If there is legal argument or matters that don't involve a jury, they will be sent home or given a late start the following morning. Jurors are usually told well in advance of any days when judges are unable to sit or have to rise early. Judges recognise that jurors must not be frightened to raise personal issues with judges, particularly in long cases. A juror must not feel inhibited about flagging up medical appointments, school prize-givings and other important events in their lives. It is important that a judge retains his ultimate authority in court, but a balance has to be drawn.

Normally the only contact barristers have with the judges presiding over their cases is in the court room itself.

Every judge has his own private room in which they will robe. Until relatively recently most courts also had a judicial dining room where all the judges would eat together. Jurors would also have their canteen where they could eat separately. However the recent cutbacks have led to the closure of many court kitchens and hot food is rarely available for anybody in court – whether judges, jurors or barristers. So nowadays everyone ends up going to the same sandwich bars close to the court building, which increases the risk of defendants and jurors bumping into each other outside court, which is undesirable for obvious reasons.

Despite the lack of communal facilities, a friendly judge will find ways of socialising. They may have a friend who is trying a case in the court room next door and spend a lot of time in and out of each other's rooms gossiping. Equally it's possible that a judge in a small court will not speak socially to anybody from the moment he arrives at court to the moment he gets home.

Just before the end of a case, after closing speeches and the summing-up, a judge may invite counsel and court officials in for tea but the case won't be discussed. Sometimes at Christmas a judge might invite counsel in for drinks. One thing no judge will ever do is to have one side in his room without the other. For obvious reasons that is simply not done.

Historically there was much more contact between judges and barristers outside of the courtroom and one of the reasons that changed is because some judges felt the need to indicate to counsel what sentence they might pass if a defendant were to plead guilty, which was not in the interests of open, transparent justice. Nowadays everyone is very strictly warned not to partake of any discussion like that, except in open court with the defendant present. If there is a meeting between judge and barristers without the defendant the clerk tape records what is said.

Inevitably judges sometimes need to discuss non-evidential matters with counsel that they don't wish to discuss in open court. For example, a juror may have suffered a family bereavement and the judge may want a steer as to whether to discharge them or adjourn the case for a few days. Or they might wish to discuss how long to take a break over Christmas and the New Year. A record will usually be made of what is said, but if the judge has confidence in counsel it may not be deemed necessary. Such meetings enable judges and barristers to speak candidly and pragmatically to each other without wasting valuable court time. Importantly, after any such meeting the defendant is always told what has happened and why, so there is no danger of him feeling that something untoward is going on behind his back.

If something goes wrong, a barrister can apply to have a judge removed from a case on the grounds that they are biased, or appear to be biased, against them or their client. This is very rarely done. Only once have I applied to have a judge recuse himself from a trial, in connection with the collapse of the property and gambling conglomerate Brent Walker. Brent Walker's founder, George Walker, and others were to be tried in two separate cases. My defendant was in the second trial, and I formed the view that the judge's comments in the first trial might give the appearance of bias. I do not believe the judge was actually biased at all but the client thought his comments were and hence I was instructed to apply to the judge to recuse himself. The judge did not accept that he had shown any bias, but he nonetheless recused himself and the case was heard by another judge.

I have never appealed a verdict on the basis that the judge was biased or acted unfairly against the defence. Such appeals do happen, rarely. In any event juries historically take against judges who appear to be biased, and tend to acquit people regardless of the evidence if they feel that the judge has been unfair.

Judges like to show that they are at least on nodding terms with modernity, and that they even have a sense of humour. Some time ago there was a case at Snaresbrook Crown Court where the clerk of the court called a defendant to his feet and asked him: 'Is your name John Smith?' – I can't remember what his actual name was — and the man replied: 'Fuckwit'.

Some judges, possibly most judges, would have sent him off to the cells for the night regardless of whether or not he was on bail and adjourned the case, but this particular judge simply turned to his clerk and asked her to amend the indictment to replace the man's name with the word 'Fuckwit'. Then asked the clerk to read the charge again . The clerk said: 'Stand up Fuckwit! Now Mr Fuckwit you're charged with this offence, how do you plead?' Apparently, he was so stunned he meekly complied and the case progressed with no further interruptions or rudeness.

CHAPTER FIFTEEN

Case 8
Private Clegg
and the Joyriders

~

When I am defending a client it is important not to get emotionally involved with them, no matter how unfair I may think it is that they find themselves in their position. While it's always important to understand how a defendant feels and to empathise with their predicament, becoming engrossed in their sense of injustice is likely to distract me from the legal task at hand and undermine my efforts to secure their acquittal.

I like to think I have always been able to defend my clients calmly and professionally regardless of what has been at stake for them — usually their liberty. There was one case, however, where I felt under considerable personal and political pressure to achieve the right result for the man sitting behind me in the dock.

Lee Clegg was a 21-year-old soldier on duty on the streets of Belfast when his life changed forever. In 1990, 20 years after the beginning of the Troubles, sectarian violence was still rife in Northern Ireland and the bloodshed would claim the lives of 81 people that year. Private Clegg would be convicted of one of those deaths.

On the evening of 30 September he and seven colleagues from the Parachute Regiment were manning a security checkpoint on the Upper Glen Road in Catholic west Belfast, as part of an anti-joyrider campaign mounted by the Royal Ulster Constabulary, the largely Protestant police force. A stolen Vauxhall Astra was driven straight at the roadblock. Fearing they were about to be the victims of a hit and run attack or a bombing, the paratroopers opened fire on the car as it bore down upon them and crashed through the roadblock without stopping. Forty shots were fired, 19 of which hit the vehicle. The driver Martin Peake, 17, and the backseat passenger Karen Reilly, 18, were killed. Another male passenger, Markiewicz Gorman, escaped with minor injuries.

The police investigated the shootings. The law was clear. To defend themselves the soldiers were entitled to open fire when the car was being driven at them, but after it had gone through the roadblock they were no longer under threat — and the legal position changed abruptly. If the fatal bullet had been fired then, it would be outside the rules of engagement and would amount to murder.

Detectives established that Karen Reilly had been killed by a bullet from Private Clegg's gun, but nobody could be sure exactly how she had been sitting in the backseat, nor how the fatal bullet had entered her body. Ballistic tests suggested that Private Clegg had fired at the car after it had gone through the checkpoint, when it could no longer be considered a threat. He was charged with the murder of Miss Reilly and the attempted wounding of Mr Peake.

Private Clegg's trial took place before a Diplock court, a special type of hearing in Northern Ireland. Diplock Courts had no jury because paramilitaries had intimidated jurors trying previous cases involving the British security forces. A solitary judge would decide Private Clegg's guilt or innocence.

At Belfast Crown Court, the judge concluded from the forensic evidence that the fatal bullet had gone through the boot, rather than the side of the car and entered the back passenger section where it had killed Miss Reilly, and that, therefore, Private Clegg had used 'lethal force without lawful purpose'. He was given a life sentence for murder with a minimum tariff of five years.

The decision enraged the British press which complained that a young man had been vilified for doing his duty. Every edition of *The Daily Mail* carried a black box recording the number of days Private Clegg had been locked up. Appeals to the Court of Appeal and House of Lords were refused, but following efforts by his supporters, including Conservative MPs and former Parachute Regiment officers, a series of fresh ballistics tests were commissioned from a renowned firearms experts, along with a new report from a leading pathologist.

The new tests were incredibly detailed and involved firing a huge number of bullets into car parts and dead pigs (which were used because of their similarity to the human body.) They showed that as the bullets penetrated the bodywork of the Astra their trajectory would have changed, making it almost impossible to say whether the fatal shot had passed through a side door or the boot.

After considering the new evidence, the Criminal Cases Review Commission referred the case back to the Court of Appeal, which quashed Private Clegg's conviction and ordered a fresh trial to test the new forensic evidence. Private Clegg was released from prison, prompting riots in Catholic areas of Belfast.

The retrial would be long and complex. Tony Scrivener, the QC who defended Private Clegg the first time, had commitments in Hong Kong at the time the case was scheduled to start in March 1999. Tony and I knew each other socially and he recommended me to Simon Mackay, Private Clegg's solicitor.

By the time the second trial came around the finishing touches were being made to the Good Friday Agreement and the Troubles had receded. I flew to Belfast to represent Private Clegg with my junior, Keir Starmer, who later became Director of Public Prosecutions and a Labour MP.

Keir had been selected, just as I had, by Private Clegg's solicitors. Solicitors want to hire the best team for their client, so they brief people they think will work well together. Sometimes they will sound you out about a potential junior and ask whether you would be happy with them. In a big criminal case strong bonds of loyalty form in a team. The case can take over the life of everyone on it and that can be good and bad. I have seen barristers become so absorbed in a trial that they have lost judgement and behaved so poorly that there have been complaints of professional misconduct. You need to get on with your junior, especially in a high-pressure case.

Fortunately, Keir was an extremely good lawyer, good company, and an excellent junior. Which was just as well because he and I lived cheek by jowl in Belfast for three months, returning to England only at weekends. After the court rose each afternoon we would go back to our base at the Hilton Hotel, have a cup of tea and a shower and meet up in a huge conference room where we worked nightly from 6pm to about 8pm. The room was packed full of car part exhibits that we used to demonstrate the new ballistics evidence on which our case was almost entirely based.

Although Private Clegg was going to give evidence and be cross-examined, in a funny way the case didn't really involve him very much. We occasionally had conferences with him and Keir went over to the British Army barracks where he was staying and played football with him and his fellow soldiers.

Keir and I would play squash once a week — I would give him the run-around on the court — and go out for a drink and dinner every night. We never dined in the hotel. We wanted to see a bit of Belfast and sample the local nightlife. We also needed a break from our routine. We frequented a few regular restaurants and Bishop's famous fish and chip shop. During breakfast on our second day at the hotel, I asked one of the waiters if I could have some fresh toast. The staff were excellent, but it was their custom to put trays of toast out at 7am and never make any more, and by 8am it was like cardboard. The waiter pointed over to the trays but I wasn't having any of it so I said: 'I don't want that, I'd like fresh toast.' Without too much trouble we were then provided with fresh toast and thereafter we continued to request it every day.

In many ways, it was quite an odd trial. While there were comparatively few security incidents while we were in Belfast and I never really felt threatened, the atmosphere was tense at times. Our solicitor agent, Donal Murphy, a Catholic, would come out with us at night, saying he was needed to make sure Keir and I didn't wander into any areas where we shouldn't, like the Falls Road, a staunchly nationalist area.

Private Clegg was on unconditional bail throughout the re-trial but, for his own protection, was brought to court under armed guard every day. He even remained under guard over lunch.

The press benches and the public gallery were packed

every day. That gets the adrenalin going more than being at Ipswich Crown Court without even a representative from the *East Anglian Daily Times* in attendance. It's also helpful for one's professional reputation. Everyone likes to see their name in print — as long as it's for the right reasons. Whenever the Irish papers referred to me in their daily coverage of the re-trial they always added the words 'who is not related to the defendant' in brackets.

The court felt very different without a jury and required a different style of advocacy. I found addressing a Diplock court much more akin to appearing at the Court of Appeal than in a normal jury trial. The judge, Mr Justice Kerr (who now sits in the Supreme Court as Lord Kerr), was not going to be swayed by rhetoric. I didn't have to explain everything to him in the same way I would to a jury, and he had read all my ballistics and forensic evidence so he already understood the points I was making.

It was very important for me to establish a good rapport with him because I was up against a Northern Ireland silk, Reg Weir (now Lord Justice Weir), who probably knew him personally. There was even a chance they were at school together. Belfast has a tiny profession and everyone knows everyone else. As an outsider I wanted to establish my bona fides early. Being a London-based QC well known at the Old Bailey wouldn't necessarily make me popular with the local Bar, so I vowed before the trial to get on with its members. Early on in the proceedings I invited the prosecutor and his junior and their wives out to dinner in order to establish cordial relations. I also joined the Northern Irish Bar Library and paid my dues so that I could use their robing room, and made a point of going into their Bar Mess to have coffee every day. As it was the barristers made me very welcome, whereas it soon emerged that my predecessor, Tony, had made himself deeply unpopular. Tony could be curmudgeonly sometimes, and the Northern Irish barristers told me that instead of joining their library so he could robe with them he had opted instead to get changed on the stairs at the court. He didn't socialise with them and I think they were pleasantly surprised by my approach.

The case was always going to turn on the ballistics evidence. Fortunately, I was able to call Graham Renshaw, a respected firearms expert, whose evidence provided the bulk of my defence case. He had worked for the Metropolitan Police's forensic science laboratory before setting up on his own and had previously worked for prosecution and defence teams. In Dr Renshaw's opinion, the bullet that killed Karen Reilly had come through the car's rear side door (with Private Clegg parallel) rather than the boot. Dr Renshaw was quietly spoken and came across as thoroughly professional. We had carried out far more ballistics reconstructions than the prosecution.

Analysing in minute detail whether or not a trigger had been pulled one second or two after a stolen car had smashed through an army checkpoint seemed to me to be a totally artificial way of deciding whether someone was guilty of murder. I shared Private Clegg's sense of injustice. Coupled with the intense political interest in the outcome of the case, I felt real pressure to get a result. Had he been found guilty for a second time the judge would have been obliged to sentence him to life in jail.

Legally a defendant convicted at a re-trial cannot receive a tougher sentence than they received at their first trial. Private Clegg had been released on licence half way through his five-year tariff, so he could not have been given more than a five year tariff. But he might still have had to go back to jail for days before the Secretary of State for Northern Ireland authorised his release.

I felt this was hugely unjust, so I wrote to Mo Mowlam MP, the then Northern Ireland Secretary, pointing out that having already been released, it would be unfair for Private Clegg to be locked up for even one more day. I implored her to set up some mechanism whereby his minimum term could be agreed in advance by the Home Secretary to allow his instant release, or alternatively for him to be given some sort of executive bail pending the Home Secretary's decision.

Out of courtesy I gave a copy of the letter to the Director of Public Prosecutions for Northern Ireland, only to find it published in the Belfast papers the following day under headlines suggesting that I thought my client was going to be convicted, which was utter nonsense. I was furious. I made a formal complaint, but I was assured by Mo Mowlam's office that they hadn't leaked it and by the DPP for NI's office that they hadn't leaked it either. It looked as though the only person left was me — and I definitely hadn't leaked it. Fortunately, I had told Private Clegg about the letter in advance and explained to him my reasons for sending it, but I was still left having to explain to him that the papers' interpretations of my motive for writing it were completely wrong.

Mr Justice Kerr retired for a long time at the end of the evidence. Then came judgement day. Slowly. In a Diplock court, the judge would review the evidence and set out his reasoning before revealing his verdict. Mr Justice Kerr was inscrutable while reading out the judgment, which spanned 189 pages. It took five hours to read out. I think some judges deliberately avoid giving any clues to their verdict until the very end to keep everyone attentive and guessing for as long as they possibly can. It's an art.

We sat listening to the judgment all morning without knowing the verdict. During the lunchtime break Private Clegg — his life stretching in front of him — and I went and had a sandwich. I don't think we were ever completely confident there would be an acquittal until the last 10 minutes of the afternoon session. Finally, Mr Justice Kerr said 'Not Guilty' to the charge of murdering Karen Reilly. However, he upheld Private Clegg's conviction on the lesser charge of wounding the driver of the stolen car (which was finally quashed by the Northern Irish Appeal Court on 31 January 2000, exonerating him completely).

After the verdict Private Clegg was quite subdued. Like

many people who get involved in notorious cases he was a bit overwhelmed by the publicity and interest. He came from a perfectly ordinary background and was being written about in every newspaper. There is no doubt that he felt he was the victim of an injustice, and I imagine that he felt that he should never have served any time in prison in the first place, time that he would never get back.

From my point of view securing his acquittal was a feather in my cap and Tony Scrivener was good enough to phone me later that day to congratulate me on the verdict. He was very pleased. The outcome was a great relief and I felt a palpable release of pressure, the like of which I had not previously experienced in any of the cases I have fought — and haven't since.

It wasn't the only victory I achieved while in Belfast, however, as I had also been responsible for the favourable outcome of the Hilton Hotel 'Toast War'. Within a fortnight of my raising the dearth of fresh toast with the hotel staff every guest was asking for and receiving fresh toast to order and they stopped putting it out at the beginning of breakfast service. It was a victory almost as satisfying as Private Clegg's acquittal.

CHAPTER SIXTEEN

How to Appeal to a Jury

~

Much of my time I am in my small office in London, poring over emails, files, reports and witness statements. When I step into court, however, I become less like a detective reading documents and more of a performer. If advocacy is likened to acting, the jury is my audience.

In a criminal trial at the crown court a professional judge decides the points of law; 12 ordinary jurors called at random from the local residents decide the verdict. Consequently, in the theatre of a courtroom, the most important people are not the judges, but the jurors. They are much more important than the judge. When I am presenting my client's case in court I never focus on the judge. By contrast I study the jury intently and tailor what I say to take account of their needs and moods.

I am conscious that anything I do or say will be seen by

the jury and they will be looking at me all the time that I am in court. If I am always getting to my feet to object to things I must consider that it may create the impression in the jury's minds that I am trying to suppress evidence. So I have to weigh up whether it is worth intervening. It may be that I think a certain question shouldn't have been asked of a witness, but if it probably hasn't done any damage I may be better off keeping quiet.

On other occasions it may be necessary to intervene immediately because there is potential for real harm to be done. In those instances, I have to be careful to object in a way that is not going to antagonise anybody. By far the best way is to get to my feet and say: 'My Lord I think there is a short point of law that needs determining and I suspect the jury would welcome the opportunity for a cup of coffee', whereupon the jury can usually barely contain their urge to escape from the stuffy surroundings. A well-timed suggestion for a break always goes down well with jurors.

As a defence lawyer, I must do three things if I am to win over the jury. Firstly, if I am to have any hope of convincing them, I must make my case intelligible. Preparing a fraud or a murder case for trial in the Crown Court can involve sifting through vast amounts of paperwork and consulting previous cases in law books. A single fraud case, for instance, may result in over 100 very thick binders stuffed with information: charges, statements, chronologies, expert witness reports; a good proportion of which may use legal terminology or technical language aimed at a professional reader. This is no good for a jury. The facts of the case must be set out in a way that a lay person can understand. I like to break down a case into its simplest components and construct a case from these simple blocks.

Secondly, if I am to make any headway, my case has to be credible. There is no point making a series of outlandish claims that no sane person would believe. My argument must make sense. It must hang together and be possible. If I have a case that is both intelligible and credible then I have a chance.

Thirdly, I must make my case interesting. Because if the jury are interested they are going to pay more attention to me than if I am boring.

Presenting a case to a jury requires careful preparation. Questioning prosecution witnesses is only half the job. I have to present my own defence witnesses. Normally I will call my client to go into the witness box. If the defendant does not give evidence the judge may inform the jury that they can draw an inference from their refusal to do so. Inevitably a jury will wonder why an innocent man or woman would not want to tell his side of the story. So in most cases I call my client to give evidence. (Though not all cases, as shown in this book).

When taking my client through their evidence in chief, a barrister must not ask a 'leading question' which is any question that can, in some way, suggest the hoped-for answer. For example, 'Was it dark?' or 'Was he carrying a gun?' are leading questions. Yet they get asked all the time. Hardly a day goes by in any case without a barrister getting to their feet to object to the way in which their opposite number is 'leading' a witness. A small number of barristers ask leading questions because they are incompetent and don't know how to avoid them. Others have just got lazy or fallen into bad habits. Some know full well that they are trampling on court protocols, but do so during important moments in the belief that it strengthens their case.

Oddly enough the prohibition on asking leading questions is a legal convention rather than a law. If you can get away without asking them, or being admonished by the judge for doing so, it often makes a much better impression with jurors. Being continually pulled up for asking leading questions looks bad in front of the jury. Sometimes barristers get away with it, either because the judge is feeling lax or is wary of intervening too often for fear of appearing to be unfair to a barrister. Sometimes judges will only haul up a barrister once the jurors have left the room.

If an opponent's habit of asking leading questions is irksome, I tend not to raise the stakes by complaining in agonised tones to the judge. Instead I might just say: 'My Lord, My Learned Friend has been around long enough to know he or she can't ask questions like that' after which everyone will have a little smile and carry on. The point has been made without any drama.

The classically correct way to obtain an account of events from a witness is to ask what are often referred to as 'W' questions – for example 'What did you see?', 'Where were you?' or 'What happened next?' Generally questions that begin with the words 'Did you?' are to be avoided as they will inevitably be leading questions.

During evidence in chief barristers often use 'piggybacking', in other words, using the witness's last answer to formulate your next question. For example, I might ask 'Where were you?' and get the reply 'I was on the pavement'. Then I'll ask: 'When you were on the pavement what way were you facing?', and so on. I can't ask 'Were you standing on the pavement?' as this would be a leading question. In practice, where there is no dispute between the two sides you can be permitted to lead a witness into a question using agreed information, for example: 'It's common ground that you were in the Pig & Whistle pub that night, what time did you arrive there?'

Cross-examination is a completely different beast to questioning your own witnesses. When cross-examining the other side's witnesses, you are permitted to ask a leading question in order to suggest an answer. You might say 'You had a gun in your hand, didn't you?' even if that was in dispute. The answer may well be 'No I didn't have a gun! The other chap had a gun. I was running, as you would have done if you'd been there!'

When you are confident of being able to contradict them, you can get a witness in chief to confirm their evidence and repeat it before then hitting them with a question like 'Are you sure about that?'. Then when you adduce the evidence which contradicts the witness you will have a powerful point to make to the jury. You have to tailor your approach to the individual case, the particular witness and any number of different factors. The object of the exercise is to hold the witness's account of what happened up to the most rigorous scrutiny, but not necessarily in a way that puts them in a bad light, so it helps to have a velvet glove as well as a flash of steel in your armoury.

The alleged victims of rapes and sexual assaults are difficult to cross-examine. The last thing I want to do is to upset them, even if certain aspects of my cross-examination — for example, the need to suggest they might be mistaken about certain things — will inevitably do just that. Nothing is more likely to get the jury on the side of such a witness than the sight of a barrister bullying them while they are on oath. It's normally best to adopt a sympathetic approach.

Sometimes confronting a witness is not just unavoidable, but essential. That is when you need a ruthless streak. I once appeared in a complicated abuse of process hearing in Liverpool that lasted for about three months and focused on H.M. Customs and Excise's use of informants to uncover alleged VAT frauds. It involved an organisation called the London City Bond and became something of a cause celebre. The crucial prosecution witness was a customs officer. I had spent a very long time preparing to cross-examine him, sifting through thousands of documents. My cross-examination revealed that one of the directors of the London City Bond was an unregistered confidential informant to the taxman. H.M. Customs and Excise had ignored its own rules on registering informants. Soon afterwards the prosecution abandoned the case against all the defendants. But it didn't stop there. The trial's collapse had a chain reaction on other cases involving the same bonded warehouse. People previously found guilty were allowed to appeal their convictions and pending cases were dropped. Tens of millions of pounds turned on my cross-examination.

You can always tell when a cross-examination is effective because the court becomes like a theatre. A room containing 60, 80 or 100 people will fall totally silent. You can almost feel the electricity in the air.

Re-examination is the last of the three phases in the questioning of a witness. After the barristers for the other parties have finished examining your witness, you can ask some more questions. If you get it right you can repair most if not all of the damage your opponents have done. But you should only re-examine a witness if it is really necessary. It's astonishing how often a witness who has just finished being cross-examined mentally collapses, thinking their ordeal is over and they no longer need to concentrate. Before you know where you are they've given some stupid answer to an innocent question and you have to spend ages on a damage limitation exercise, until hopefully, the jury forget what has been said.

When I am examining, cross-examining, re-examining or making a closing speech, I try to pick up the vibes from the jury. Some jurors are easy to read from their facial expressions and how they react physically to what is being said. They may nod when they agree with a point, make a point of writing down a note and also clearly indicate disagreement if that is the position. If they are interested, they may lean forward and make notes, or nudge each other and pick up the bundles of case papers. If jurors are obviously engaged in a particular point you may as well slow down in order to emphasise it further and even go over it again. I may flatter an alert jury by saying: 'It was perfectly obvious how you noticed the importance of that identifying witness. We could see you making notes. It was plain to see that the description was very different from the description you were given a few minutes before.'

On the other hand jaundiced jurors may raise their eyes or whisper audibly to the person next door: 'Oh, not this again.' If I get the impression that the jury think I am making a duff point it's probably wise to move on. That's not always possible, of course. Sometimes I must plough on with a line of questioning, even though the jury are bored. But I might acknowledge that the next day by saying: 'Yesterday afternoon was pretty slow-going and tedious, if not boring, but in fact it was very important for these reasons, so don't write it off. Just focus on these aspects and all will become clear later.'

I pay special care to my closing speech. It is the last part of my case that the jury will hear before they retire to consider their verdicts. Closing speeches can take up the best part of a day, and take place before the judge sums up, when he runs through the main points of the case and highlights the most salient evidence. The purpose of a barrister's closing speech is not to summarise what the jury have heard during the trial, but to make the argument as to why your client is not guilty. Humility is helpful. In some circumstances humour may lighten the load. As an advocate, I want the jury to warm to me.

When the jury retire, there is no set time for them to return. Waiting for the jury to come back is nerve-wracking for the client, whose whole life will be changed by the words: 'Guilty' or 'Not Guilty'. I never tell the client which way I think the verdict will go. I obviously don't want to tell them that I think they will be found guilty. Alternatively, I don't want to say that I think they will be 'Not Guilty' in case the verdict goes the other way. About 80 to 90 per cent of the time the verdict is the one I expected. I have disagreed with some verdicts but I wouldn't say they were surprising or harsh. Even the ones I got wrong, I can see why the jury might have come to that conclusion.

Generally I think juries do a good job. I would rather have a criminal case decided by ordinary people than by lawyers. Barristers aren't actually trained to assess people's character or their truthfulness, but jurors are. They are trained as they go about their ordinary business. Throughout life they have to decide: do I believe what this neighbour is saying, do I believe what this salesman is selling, do I accept what this politician is telling me? Jurors have got all the experience necessary to be able to decide whether someone is telling the truth. By contrast, lawyers are too cynical to make these decisions. We suffer from the 'I've heard it all before' syndrome, where we don't spot the person who is telling the truth because we have seen so many liars.

Juries are much more likely to come to the right result. Everybody in the legal profession is constantly impressed by their conscientiousness. We have had juries in one form or another since the 13th Century and they are probably the best system: 12 ordinary people using their common sense and judgement to work out what really happened. What's the alternative?

CHAPTER SEVENTEEN

Case 9
Don Banfield:
A Murder Without a Body?

~

Most members of the public assume that the police must have a dead body before making an accusation of murder. In fact, it is possible to secure a conviction for murder without finding a body. In such circumstances the evidence necessarily must be strong, otherwise we could all make serious accusations about people we haven't seen for a while.

In Don Banfield's case, the evidence was not strong — it was just puzzling. In 2001 Mr Banfield, 63, had just retired as the manager of a betting shop in Hampstead, north London. One day he had gone to his local police station and told them: 'I think my wife is trying to kill me'. He told officers there was something wrong with the food Shirley, 53, had been preparing for him and suspected she was trying to poison him. He also said he had once woken up to find his wife trying to smother him with a pillow. Mr Banfield also claimed their 29-year-old daughter, Lynette, had previously brandished a large knife in his presence, causing him to reflect on his future.

Oddly perhaps for someone apparently in fear of his life, Trinidadian-born Mr Banfield went home from the station to continue living with his wife and daughter in Wealdstone, London. Perhaps because of this — or perhaps because he had previously vanished from the West Indies without warning or a forwarding address, shortly after telling friends of his desire to disappear — detectives were somewhat sceptical about his claims that Shirley wanted to do away with him.

Nonetheless, shortly after he visited the police station Mr Banfield did disappear. His friends realised he wasn't around and alerted the police. Officers went to see Shirley who told them that she hadn't reported him missing because he often went on a 'bender' for days at a time. In the absence of any evidence that Mr Banfield had come to harm the police logged him as a missing person and that was the end of the matter, until detectives conducted a cold case review in July 2009. They discovered that Mr Banfield had received a large cash sum after being made redundant from his employers William Hill shortly before his disappearance. He had also signed a contract for the sale of the family home which would have realised a £120,000 profit, which he intended to split with his wife before they went their separate ways. After he vanished, his share of the proceeds remained untouched. Shirley, however, had fraudulently continued to collect his pension by making various representations to the effect that he was alive and well. She tried to justify this to police by claiming that her husband had returned home out of the blue one Christmas before leaving again.

Early in 2011 detectives handed a new file to the Crown Prosecution Service who decided to prosecute Mr Banfield's wife and his daughter for his murder. I was retained to represent Shirley Banfield. I and Lynette Banfield's legal teams believed it was an open and shut case.

The prosecution had no body and no actual time, place or mechanism of death. Not only was there no proof that Mr Banfield was dead, there were several tantalising hints that he was in fact still alive, including a number of alleged sightings, one of which came from a policewoman. We naturally made the most of this evidence during the ensuing month-long trial at the Old Bailey in March 2012.

We presented the case to the jury in two alternative ways. Firstly, we argued that there was no evidence from which a jury could be sure that Mr Banfield was dead. Secondly, we argued 'in the alternative' that if he was dead there was no evidence who had killed him or where or how he was killed.

At 'half-time' after the prosecution case ended, we asked the judge to abandon the case. We pointed out that if Mr Banfield had been killed, then it could not be proved which of the two defendants had done it, and whether it was one of them acting alone or both together. In those circumstances they should both be found not guilty, we said. The judge declined to stop the case.

Despite the prosecution's case being wholly circumstantial, the jury found both women guilty and they were sentenced to life imprisonment in April 2012. Mrs Banfield was given a minimum term of 18 years and her daughter 16 years.

Both women appealed and I was retained to represent Mrs Banfield for her appeal. I was about as confident as I could be that I would overturn her conviction.

Although there was no concession that he had been killed by someone at the trial, the jury's verdict made it obvious that they believed Mr Banfield had been murdered. There were also several factors which pointed to him being dead. If he was alive, why hadn't he asked his former employers to re-direct his pension to him? And why hadn't he collected his share of the proceeds from the sale of the house?

So, pragmatically, at the appeal we accepted Mr Banfield had been murdered. However accepting that didn't help the prosecution prove that he had been killed by his wife and daughter. The only motive they could have had was to take his share of the house sale, but his share had not been touched.

We pointed out that even if we went one step further and accepted that Mr Banfield had been killed by one or both of them it did not help decide which of them had killed him.

We posed three questions. Did the evidence prove that his wife alone did it, with her daughter helping to dispose of the body afterwards? Or did the evidence prove that his daughter alone killed him with her mother helping afterwards? Or did it prove that they both acted together at all times? As far as I could see there was absolutely no evidence supporting any of those scenarios. Even assuming that one of them was correct, there was no evidence as to which one it was. But somehow the jury in their original trial had found them guilty on the basis that it was a joint enterprise — it didn't matter who had done away with him, they had both agreed to Mr Banfield's death.

In July 2013, the three judges at the Court of Appeal took the view that unless you were able to answer any of our three questions with an emphatic 'yes' you couldn't exclude the possibility that one of them had been responsible for Mr Banfield's death without the participation of the other, and that in those circumstances both of their convictions could not be safe.

The judges also took the view that the judge had been wrong not to stop the trial at the end of the prosecution case. Sometimes judges feel under pressure to let a trial run so a jury can decide guilt or innocence, even if they know the prosecution case is weak. That's understandable, but it is not right.

After the pair's convictions were quashed the CPS decided against a re-trial, wisely in my opinion. Mrs Banfield and her daughter remain free to this day. I have no idea who killed Mr Banfield, if he was killed. He might still be alive.

CHAPTER EIGHTEEN

21st Century Set

~

Michael Lewis remained Head of Chambers for 10 years until he retired in 1994. There were two obvious candidates to replace him: Howard Godfrey and me. We had taken silk on the same day and were friends, but both of us wanted the job. The obvious thing to do was to have an election, but Howard magnanimously decided that he would withdraw rather than have a vote which might prove divisive, and became my deputy. Twenty-two years after squatting at 3 Hare Court, clinging onto my place there with my fingertips, I was now Head of Chambers.

Unlike the gleaming, steel-and-glass towers that were rising into the sky all over London, in the 1990s barristers' chambers were mostly still stuck in cramped, shambling old houses in the alleys, side streets, and occasional grand road off Fleet Street. In the City of London and the upstart Canary Wharf to the east stockbrokers, traders, solicitors and accountants who made London a global centre for services sat behind sleek desks in air conditioned offices. At 3 Hare Court, we didn't even have central heating. Its warren of small single offices didn't suit a modern set of criminal barristers who were out at court most of the day, especially at the uneconomic rents we were being charged.

Despite its dilapidation, many tenants opposed the idea of moving out of 3 Hare Court, which was steeped in tradition. Judge Jeffreys, the notorious 17th Century 'Hanging Judge', had had his chambers on the site and it was viewed in equal measure with affection and trepidation. We had all been practising there since we were pupils. Some feared that if we lost the 3HC name and address we would lose work because solicitors were so used to sending briefs there.

In 1998, however, there was an opportunity to escape. The Inner Temple announced that it wanted to renovate 3 Hare Court and that we would have to move out during the refurbishments. We were decanted into cramped temporary accommodation around the corner in Essex Street. Fortunately, the move allayed fears that our caseload would shrink; the move made absolutely no difference. The Inner Temple then tipped us into action by refusing to renovate 3HC to an acceptable standard. We wanted air conditioning, the Inner Temple did not. To compound matters we were under some pressure from a chambers below to move out so that it could expand into our quarters. We could have resisted its advances, but all of a sudden a five-storey property on Bedford Row just north of High Holborn came onto the market.

This galvanised us into activating a putative plan by a member of chambers, Jim Sturman, to buy our own premises outside the Inns. The Allied Irish Bank, which was a very generous lender in the late 1990s, was willing to offer a mortgage. The tenants discussed the idea at meetings and ultimately voted to abandon 3 Hare Court and buy 2 Bedford Row. Just before we moved a few people got cold feet, but they eventually decided they were better off staying with those determined to move. All the tenants who wanted to invest in the property took out mortgages on good terms from the bank. A trust company was set up which took ownership of the building and which those who chose to invest in the building had shares in. Every tenant was invited to buy shares. Some did, some didn't.

We took possession of 2 Bedford Row in December 1999. As a building it is much better suited to a 21st Century legal practice. Barristers share desks in large rooms. We have dedicated conference rooms with video conference facilities and air conditioning.

Since we made the move, several chambers have left rooms owned by the Inns for Bedford Row, which is now described as 'The Fifth Inn'. Many sets copied our blueprint of creating a trust and used the same solicitors as we did.

Although most chambers are still located in London around the Inns of Court, sets no longer need the Inns' permission to move to new areas. Quite a few have relocated to the City of London, to be closer to the big banks. There are also sets on the outskirts of London such as Stratford and Harrow, and, as was always the case, many in major cities all over the United Kingdom.

Chambers have also grown in size. In times gone by chambers were much smaller with perhaps only seven or eight tenants and a solitary clerk each. Nowadays it's completely uneconomic to have such compact sets and many have anything from 50 to 100 or more barristers.

Lawyers tend to move more frequently between chambers nowadays. When we set up in 1984 nobody defected to another set for about 10 years. During that time other people joined us, such as John Morris QC, a minister in the governments of Harold Wilson and James Callaghan, who became Attorney General in Tony Blair's first government. Since then several of our silks have also moved on to become judges, including Mrs Justice McGowan at the High Court, His Honour Judge Dodd QC, and His Honour Judge Lodder QC, who is now the Recorder of Kingston-upon-Thames.

While our trust worked well for a long time and the mortgage was paid off, the people who had retired or left chambers to become judges wanted to recoup their investment. Unfortunately, the junior barristers who joined chambers later couldn't afford to buy shares in the trust because no bank would lend at the generous terms we enjoyed in 1999. In the end 2BR was sold to outside investors and everybody who had purchased shares was paid out... after we had given ourselves a watertight and renewable lease.

At 2 Bedford Row, we have grown in size to 70 tenants. As we have expanded so, too, has the need for more clerks to drum up a constant supply of work. We employ seven, six men and one woman. John Grimmer, that hard working junior clerk who split from the old guard at 3HC to join our 'revolution', is still our senior clerk running the clerks' room and overseeing the practices of all the tenants.

As a result of our collective efforts, 2BR is now regarded as one of the leading sets for criminal work in the country and has been for more than a decade.

Our current constitution stipulates that we must hold an election for Head of Chambers and Deputy every three years, as long as someone wants to stand against the incumbent. We've had elections for Deputy Head of Chambers, but nobody has ever stood against me.

I remain Head of Chambers to this day.

CHAPTER NINETEEN

Case 10
War Crimes in the Balkans

~

War crimes are unusual in that people who have never committed an offence of violence before engage in acts of ethnic cleansing and genocide, against their neighbours. The capacity to commit these crimes is within us all and although from the comfort of our sitting rooms we might confidently say that we would never act like that, the Nazi era and other episodes in history prove that many do. So it was in the Balkans, just a few years ago.

When President Tito of Yugoslavia died in 1990 simmering tensions between the ethnic races living in the Slavic federation burst into life and Slovenia and Croatia declared independence. The Serbian-dominated Yugoslav army sought to suppress the breakaway states until there was a UN-monitored ceasefire in 1992.

Bosnia, an ethnic mix of Croats, Muslims and Serbs, was next to seek independence. Its minority Serb population, backed by neighbouring Serbs and the Yugoslav Army (renamed the Bosnian Serb Army) fiercely resisted the demand. In the ethnic cleansing that followed more than one million Muslims and Croats were driven from their homes and over 100,000 men, women and children were killed. For the first time since the Second World War genocide, ethnic cleansing and other war crimes were visited upon mainland Europe.

Horrified by the conflict's brutality, the international community set up an international court in the Netherlands to try the perpetrators of the most egregious cruelties. Just as happenstance led me to represent Szymon Serafinowicz and then Anthony Sawoniuk, in early April 1999, I flew to the Hague to represent Duško Tadić, a Bosnian Serb, at an appeal hearing before the International Tribunal for the Former Yugoslavia at The Hague.

In 1997, while Scotland Yard was struggling to secure its first conviction for the death of Jews more than 50 years earlier, Tadić was judged to have taken part in ethnic cleansing of Muslims in Bosnia earlier that decade. In all, he had been found guilty on nine charges, partly guilty on two more and not guilty on 20. As a result, he became the first man to be convicted by an International Court of war crimes since the Nuremberg trials.

Tadić had appealed all his convictions to the Appeal Chamber. However his lead lawyer during his trial, Milan Vujin, a Serbian, was unable to act for him again after coming under suspicion of not acting in Tadić's best interests and of seeking to protect others by not pursuing evidence that might embarrass them or the Serbian government. The court's charge of contempt against Vujin was found to be proven.

In these circumstances it was obvious that Vujin could not act in the appeal. By this time, I suspect the court and Tadić wanted a lawyer who had no connection to any of the countries involved in the conflict. I had had experience of war crimes cases, albeit in the English courts. I also had the distinct advantage of having a barrister in chambers, John Livingston, who spoke Serbo-Croat and whose wife was well-connected in the former Yugoslavia; she had introduced him and then me to the case.

I met Tadić in the United Nations Detention Facility, which was a jail within a jail outside The Hague. I had to go through a Dutch jail to get to the Detention Centre where the security was provided by UN guards. It smelt of stale cabbage like all other prisons I have visited, but it was more peaceful than a normal prison, with plenty of time for visits when families could make the journey. The relaxed atmosphere was fostered by the Irish governor, who had managed to house prisoners from opposite sides of the conflict without any animosity that I could detect.

Tadić seemed to be a gentle family man. Like Serafinowicz and Sawoniuk, he was not a general or politician who had ordered troops to engage in genocide or ethnic cleansing, but a low-ranked traffic policeman who had previously been a postman. Like many others who behaved barbarously during the war, he had lived a perfectly conventional life beforehand, exhibiting no signs of racial prejudice or anti-Muslim sentiments. Once the war started, however, he joined the Serbian Paramilitary Force which murdered Muslims in cold blood solely because of their religion.

Tadić had been convicted of shooting two Muslim policemen in the head during an operation of ethnic cleansing through the territory of Prijedor in Bosnia. The Muslims in the towns and villages visited by the paramilitary force would have the men separated from the women and children and taken away to concentration camps. Frequently, though, the Muslims would receive prior warning that the paramilitaries were on their way and would evacuate to a safe place nearby. Two policemen who were Muslims were still in the town when the gunmen arrived. They were detained in the market place when Tadić was alleged to have walked up to them, put a pistol to their head and fired. This was seen by one witness, Nihad Seferović, a Muslim who had escaped before the paramilitaries arrived but returned to the village in order to feed his pet pigeons. Tadić's conviction rested on the uncorroborated evidence of Seferović alone.

Seferović had been made available as a witness to the prosecution by the government of Bosnia and Herzegovina. We suspected he may have been a plant. Another witness made available by the same government, Dragan Opačić, had been found to be untruthful in different matters and we questioned Seferovic's reliability by relying on the fact that he came from the same tainted source. We also argued that the story of Seferovic returning to a town where he risked being shot, so as to feed some pigeons, was so improbable that its accuracy was in doubt.

The prosecution was appealing Tadić's acquittal over the killing of five men in the village of Jaskici in an act of ethnic cleansing in which Tadić participated. The men had escaped the initial division of men for slaughter but been detained later. There were no witnesses at all as to who shot them.

Defending a case at the International Tribunal for the Former Yugoslavia came with a certain friseur. The camaraderie of barristers in England was starkly absent. The defence and the prosecution did not meet outside court and when I went along counsel's bench to shake hands with my opponents and introduce myself they did not know quite how to react. The defence lawyers were not invited to the canteen with the court staff and prosecutors and our computers and photocopiers were noticeably inferior. We were made to feel like second-class citizens.

In court, each counsel either wore the robes from his own country or a rather anonymous black gown; I wore the robes I wore in England but not the wig. We could listen on earphones to proceedings, which were simultaneously translated into English, French and Serbo-Croat. A live television feed was screened in court and broadcast on channels in the Netherlands and the former Yugoslavia.

Five formidable prosecutors battled us every step of the way: Upawansa Yapa, former Solicitor General of Sri Lanka, Brenda Hollis, a former colonel in the US Air Force, her compatriot Michael Keegan, Professor William Fenwick from Canada, and the Australian Ann Sutherland. John Livingston and I felt outnumbered.

On 20 January 2000, the five judges in the Appeal Chamber upheld Tadić's conviction. They overturned some of his not guilty verdicts and found him guilty of five more murders. It was a comprehensive defeat. My one success was having Tadić's 20-year sentence cut by three and a half years to take account of the time he had spent in custody in Germany before he was extradited to the United Nations Detention Centre and for the period between his trial and appeal.

After the Tadić case my next brief was the appeal of Goran Jelisić, a Bosnian Serb, who had been jailed for 40 years for crimes against humanity and violations of the laws and customs of war. Jelisić had pleaded guilty to those counts and had been acquitted of counts of genocide. He had appealed the sentence and the prosecution had appealed his acquittal for genocide.

While I fought Jelisić's case just as hard as that of any

other, I found him to be a much less sympathetic character than Tadić. In fact, he was one of the most evil people I have ever met. Personally, I found him chilling. He seemed to be completely without emotion or feelings. Before the war he had been a farm mechanic. He was married and had a son. During the war, he was an officer at the Luka concentration camp where many hundreds of Muslims were tortured and killed. Jelisić admitted taking an active and leading part in the killings. He did not help his case by referring to himself as Adolf the Second and stating that he wanted to rid the world of Muslims like one cleans one's head of lice. The judges upheld his 40 year term.

No sooner had I concluded his case than I was instructed to act in an appeal for Drago Josipović, a Bosnian Croat who was convicted with four others of carrying out a blood-curdling attack on Ahmici, a small village in central Bosnia on 16 April 1993. More than 100 civilian Muslim men, women and children were killed in the assault, which was part of a rampage by the Croatian Military Police known as The Jokers through Muslim settlements in the Lasla valley. All 169 Muslim houses in the village were destroyed, along with two mosques. Not a single Croat home was touched.

At the original sentencing of Josipović and his four accomplices in January 2000, the tribunal's presiding judge, Antonio Cassese, put the violence and barbarity into its historic context, when he said:

> Indisputably, what happened on 16 April 1993, in Ahmici has gone down in history as comprising one of the most vicious illustrations of man's inhumanity to man... [its] name must be added to the long list of previously unknown hamlets and towns that recall abhorrent misdeeds and make us all shudder with horror and shame: Dachau, Oradour sur Glane, Katijn, Mazabotto, Soweto, My Lai, Sabra and Shatila and so many others.

Josipović had been jailed for 15 years for participating in the arson of civilian homes and the murder of at least three Muslims, including a 14-year-old child. I led in his appeal, which was dismissed in 2001. However his sentence was reduced to 12 years, because there was no proof he had been in a position of command during the attack.

Before the war Josipović and his colleagues had lived peaceably in Bosnia all their lives. They had been shopkeepers, factory workers and the like and had lived alongside their Muslim neighbours in harmony. Josipović himself had worked in a chemicals factory.

In the Balkan war crimes cases and particularly Josipović's, something that I had observed in my Second World War war crimes trials really hit home: namely that the people who commit crimes against humanity are frequently people who have never behaved in an anti-social way before and had they not been placed in the position they were, they would never have done anything anti-social, let alone commit murder. The trials taught me that it is within everyone to behave in a way that involves the commission of crimes against humanity and no-one can predict how they will react unless they are placed in that situation. Most of my war crimes defendants were ordinary people who had found themselves in an extraordinary position and reacted, whether because of peer pressure or propaganda or for other reasons, in a way that they could never had imagined before the conflict.

CHAPTER TWENTY

Inside Chambers: Rivalry and Camaraderie

~

Being Head of Chambers is like being the chief executive of a small company. About 90 people work at 2 Bedford Row: barristers, clerks, administrative staff, and cleaners. Our running costs, including rent, rates, wages, heating, electricity, IT and technical support, and pupillage awards, are £2.2 million a year.

That keeps me busy. During the week I will wake up at 6am in my two-bedroom flat at Gray's Inn. I will have a quick shower, shave and a cup of tea and be at my desk in chambers at 6.30am. In the next three hours I get more work done than in the following six; there are no telephone calls, no staff, no interruptions. No nothing. I read papers, draft opinions and prepare questions for cases, and perhaps answer emails, which arrive in their hundreds daily.

When everyone else arrives at 9.30am, the work is the same, but slower. The chambers' accountant will come in with a query about a bill or suggest we move to a new supplier, or the administrator will ask about some regulation from the Bar Council that someone may not have followed, or the receptionist will phone in sick and I must decide whether to get a temp.

To fund our overheads, barristers pay dues into chambers according to their income and seniority. Anyone who has been at the Bar for less than five years pays £3,000-a-year, more than five years and it's £6,000-a-year. Over 10 years the rent is £9,000-a-year. For QCs it's £12,000-a-year.

However, barrister's rent only makes up a small proportion of our income. The majority comes from taking a percentage of tenants' earnings. Each barrister pays 11 per cent of their fees back into chambers to cover running costs. If somebody can't pay their rent, perhaps because they've been seriously ill, I will recommend that the management committee waive it until they are back at work.

Chambers is quite like a family. Once a barrister is a member they are a member for the rest of their career unless they are found guilty of a criminal offence or serious professional misconduct. We would never get rid of a barrister because their practice wasn't thriving. Criticising a member of chambers for earning too little is also not the done thing, but as Head of Chambers I am obliged to intervene if a tenant is doing sub-standard work, perhaps as a result of illness or domestic problems.

An informal network of support exists within the law and other barristers will let us know if someone is failing in court. They might phone up completely confidentially and say: 'Look X was in court today and he clearly wasn't himself.' Or a judge might phone me up and say: 'Look I had Y in front of me and he clearly wasn't himself. Maybe you should have a word with him and see if there's a problem?'

Depression is the most common problem. On very rare occasions, I have had to say to a tenant that I felt they weren't well enough to be working and that perhaps they ought to take a month or two off and seek counselling or some other help. Oddly enough, I often find that the person is incredibly relieved that someone else has taken the initiative rather than them feeling they have to keep going even when they don't feel up to it. Rather than resenting the intervention, they are grateful for it.

Even if people are not earning lots, there is a role for them in chambers. Less busy tenants can do the smaller cases that always need covering. I have never felt that one of our tenants, in good health, was unable to do a case competently or well, which partly reflects our selection process for new tenants and our position in the market.

Barristers very seldom coast along without putting in much work, although it is possible to do so. What I sometimes have to deal with, however, is barristers who aren't as successful as they should be, or would like to be. When there is not enough work to go around, tenants tend to blame people other than themselves. No barrister has ever come to me and said: 'I'm not doing very well because I'm not very good.' They always say: 'I'm not doing very well because that clerk is useless or because this idiot solicitor didn't do that, or that judge has got it in for me.'

In my view there is no point a barrister blaming the clerks for not supplying them with enough lucrative work. The solicitor and the client choose the barrister, not the clerk. No solicitor is going to come in with a brief worth £1,000 and tell the clerks to give it to who they want. Nonetheless junior members sometimes think the senior clerk is channelling all the best paid work to the silks and complain: 'I haven't had a decent case for ages.' I might be Head of Chambers but I have to be diplomatic.

If a barrister feels particularly aggrieved, we may arrange for them to have a meeting with the senior clerk, with a view to building up their caseload. The clerk might say: 'You have been getting some work from X and Y solicitors, we could make a plan perhaps for trying to build up a relationship with them, so that you're not the third or fourth choice for that firm but perhaps the first or second.'

Some may feel a little cautious about calling for such a meeting for fear it will be construed as a personal attack on the integrity of the senior clerk or his juniors. This is not the case, though in my experience the clerks are fairly even-handed.

In reality, things are often the other way around: some

barristers have so much work that they simply can't do it all. Inevitably in those situations you will get solicitors who try to interest you in cases which are not going to pay as much as you would ordinarily charge simply because they are so interesting. They might only be providing you with three-quarters of your normal fee, but the solicitor will tell you that you really ought to take the case because it will be good for your career. It's a way of getting you to do cases that you would not normally do.

Spotting the tenants who have great talent and who will eventually take silk is easy. I can tell by the level of work they are getting, how they conduct themselves in court, and what solicitors say about their performance. I can also identify those who never will. The difficult category is those who might take silk.

When a tenant says they want to make an application for silk I often put their aspirations to the test by asking them how many (and which) solicitors brief them regularly, and how much of the work they are doing now will they still be able to do if they become a QC. If there is any uncertainty in their reply I ask them: 'Ask yourself this, if you take silk where is the work going to come from to support you?' A confident junior barrister might point out to me that they already have nine months work which should be done by a silk, which would make them an obvious candidate to apply.

I also have to manage the expectations of those who I think are less well placed. If a barrister in our set wants to take silk and I don't think they're ready for it, I have a duty to say so and to explain my concerns. A new QC who fails to get work can spiral downwards into bankruptcy.

A chambers is home to rivalry and jealousy and inevitably there can be strains between the highest and lowest-earning barristers. Cuts in Legal Aid fees have exacerbated these tensions. A junior barrister who is doing good quality Legal Aid work will earn less than £70-an-hour, which is less than a plumber. Out of that £70-an-hour they have to pay their rent, 11 per cent to chambers, travel costs and all their other expenses. The barrister doing the same work in the private market will charge several times that Legal Aid rate. This means that some barristers are paying a disproportionate amount of rent to subsidise those whose income, through no fault of their own, has been slashed by the government.

It's much better if everyone in chambers gets on, but there are people who don't. Some advocates rub each other up the wrong way and things can lead to them falling out. I have known cases where silks in the same chambers have ended up not speaking to each other during cases and have communicated by writing notes. In these situations, I have had to intervene and tell them to grow up. This doesn't happen very often but when it does it's usually because disagreements between barristers on opposing sides have been taken personally. The defence lawyer might feel the prosecutor is being unfair, the prosecutor is insulted by the accusation and the whole thing escalates.

As Head of Chambers I am responsible for ensuring that members of my chambers operate within the rules of our profession, renew their practising certificates, and are insured. In practice the chambers' administrator carries out this function, but if anybody isn't meeting their obligations they are referred to me.

An independent body, the Bar Standards Board, regulates all barristers using a code of conduct. Most of its cases concern barristers who have not complied with their professional development obligations. They are usually given a deadline and a fine of a few hundred pounds.

However, some more serious cases involve a barrister's behaviour in court. Judges have reported barristers to the Bar Standards Board for being rude or insulting, failing to comply with rulings they have given, or misconducting themselves by failing to comply with the rules that govern their field of advocacy. For example, barristers who intend to argue a particular point in court are obliged to forewarn the other side. Breaching that obligation can become the subject of professional disciplinary proceedings, as can other misconduct, such as failing to turn up for hearings without a valid excuse.

In 2014 I and a junior, David Patience, represented a barrister from another chambers, Lawrence McNulty, who was reported by his judge to the Bar Standards Board for his conduct of a big terrorism trial at Manchester Crown Court in 2011, R v Farooqi & Others. The defendants were ultimately convicted of encouraging vulnerable members of their community to join jihad in Afghanistan and Pakistan.

Mr McNulty was accused of making submissions to the jury regarding entrapment, in direct contravention of a ruling by the judge, Mr Justice Henriques, that entrapment was not a defence open to his client. During his closing speech Mr McNulty also likened the judge to a secondhand car salesman and impugned the reputation of a witness without having put the allegations to him in the witness box.

He felt strongly his client wasn't getting a fair trial, but a barrister must accept the judge's rulings. If you think they are wrong, you can use them as grounds for an appeal later if appropriate. The trouble is people can get tunnel-vision in big cases when they are under intense pressure.

Mr McNulty denied presenting legal argument as evidence during his closing speech, claiming he was merely not expressing himself very well. He argued that although he had got close to transgressing the judge's ruling he hadn't actually done so, and that when he called the judge a secondhand car salesman he was just using an analogy that would convey to jurors the point he was trying to make. Personally, I am confident that if the only transgression had been referring to the judge as a second hand car salesman there would have been no formal complaint. The trouble was it was one of a number of transgressions.

Mr McNulty was convicted of four of five charges. He

was, however, acquitted of presenting argument as evidence. He was suspended from practice for four months, which was a good result because many people expected him to be disbarred.

Many people thought he had made a very serious professional error and that clients wouldn't want to instruct him again, but some solicitors would think: 'He gave the judge a bloody nose, he stood up to him', so it hasn't wrecked his practice. Undoubtedly he thought he was giving his client the best defence. My view is that the rules must be followed, otherwise proceedings become a free-for-all. Looking back, I don't think anyone behaved particularly well at that trial. I would never have acted in court like Mr McNulty, but I had to do my utmost to defend him; I had to look at the case through his eyes.

I also gave evidence in a case where a barrister was sued over his conduct during a rape trial at which the defendant was convicted. The barrister had advised the defendant that he had no grounds of appeal. He served five years before being released but his time inside hadn't diminished his burning sense of injustice and he went to one of the newspapers, which subsequently contacted me for a second opinion on his case. When I saw the papers, I decided that he had very real grounds for appeal against his conviction. I settled grounds for appeal and the conviction was later quashed. A retrial was ordered at which he was acquitted but he never got any compensation from the state. He went on to sue the barrister for negligence and I had to give evidence against my fellow professional in the resulting civil action.

Barristers can also be hauled up for things they have allegedly done outside court that discredit the legal profession. A barrister convicted of theft, for instance, would almost certainly be disbarred which would mean that he could never practise again as a barrister, while a conviction for drink driving might only warrant a reprimand. Recently a newspaper exposed one barrister as a male escort, but nothing has happened to him; I don't think anyone reported him to the Bar Standards Board.

In all my 46 years of practising I have only been the subject of one complaint, for allegedly making a comment on the BBC *Today* programme about Michael Stone's trial before it had concluded. I had actually given the interview after the verdict and the case against me was thrown out. I was never told the identity of the person who had complained about me.

Despite occasional rivalry and jealousy, I like to think that 2 Bedford Row is still a friendly place, as well as an effective one. As we have grown in size the closeness of friendships and collegiate atmosphere of earlier years have faded a little. Some people hardly ever come in to chambers, but a hard core will still drink and dine together regularly. Many tenants are friends as well as colleagues. Three or four times a year I will arrange drinks, to welcome a new tenant or perhaps just for the sheer hell of it, or we will entertain some solicitors. About once a year we will have a formal black tie dinner to which everyone and their partners are invited, normally to mark someone becoming a judge, retiring, or taking silk.

Every year on a Saturday we also have what we call a 'mock trial' where the pupils act out a trial in a real court room and the tenants sit as the jury or as ushers. I'm always the judge.

We usually adjourn to a bar afterwards.

CHAPTER TWENTY-ONE

Case 11
The Murder of Jill Dando

~

Some crimes are so heinous and depraved, so abhorrent to any human being with the merest shred of moral decency, that they are guaranteed to reignite calls for the return of the death penalty. When public emotions are running high in the aftermath of a particularly gruesome child murder, I understand why some people clamour for the reintroduction of capital punishment.

I, though, will never advocate the taking of a life to exact revenge for any crime. No matter how fine our legal system is there will always be occasional miscarriages of justice. Nothing reinforces my belief that the death penalty should stay consigned to history than the worrying case of Barry George, who was convicted of a murder he did not commit, on the flimsiest of evidence.

The cold-blooded killing of the television personality Jill Dando shocked the British public. When she died aged 37, Miss Dando was in the prime of her life and her career. She was engaged to be married and presented two of the BBC's most popular shows, *Crimewatch* and *Holiday.*

On the morning of 26 April 1999, Miss Dando had driven back to her home in Fulham, south west London, after spending the night with her fiancé, Alan Farthing, a surgeon, in nearby Chiswick. At around 11.30am a neighbour heard what he assumed to be a cry or shriek of greeting coming from outside Miss Dando's home in Gowan Avenue. Moments later he saw a six-foot-tall white man walking away from the house.

Miss Dando had been shot dead as she was about to enter her front door. Her body was discovered less than a quarter of an hour later by another horrified neighbour who alerted the police, triggering a nationwide manhunt. Media interest in the killing was frenzied. Miss Dando was television's 'girl next door': personable, photogenic and cherished by viewers.

Police were unable to establish any motive for the killing and conspiracy theories abounded. There were claims her death had been ordered by shadowy political figures in Serbia enraged by the charity appeal she had made for Kosovan refugees days earlier. It was also suggested she had been murdered on the orders of an unknown gangland boss in revenge for the role *Crimewatch* had played in bringing criminals to justice. To add to the mystery, Miss Dando's brother, Nigel, said she had recently become concerned about a man who had been pestering her.

The suggestion that her death might have been ordered from within Serbia had no credibility in my eyes. I couldn't see any point in the Serbs doing such a thing and not telling anyone afterwards. If you are going to make a political point you have to publicise it or you are wasting your time.

However, it was obvious that whoever murdered Miss Dando knew exactly what they were doing. Her killer had grabbed her from behind as she was about to put her keys in the front door and forced her down onto the ground. She was then shot in the head at point blank range. The bullet which killed her came from a 9mm automatic pistol. The murder had all the hallmarks of a professional 'hit'. No tell-tale forensic clues had been left at the scene by her killer. He (assuming it was a man) had concealed himself so effectively in her tiny front garden as he waited for her to come home that he had not been seen by anyone. Analysis of CCTV footage used to track Miss Dando's journey from her fiance's house to her own home had ruled out the possibility that she had been followed.

In the first six months of the murder inquiry detectives interviewed more than 2,500 people and took 1,000 statements, but by the turn of the year they still didn't have a suspect. In May 2000, more than a year after the murder, their focus turned to Barry George, a 40-year-old loner who called himself Barry Bulsara after adopting the real surname of the late Queen singer Freddie Mercury.

A failed Territorial Army recruit, Barry lived near Miss Dando in Fulham. He had a history of adopting the names of famous rock stars and once tried to pass himself off as an ex-member of the SAS who had been involved in the Iranian Embassy siege. He had a spent conviction for impersonating a police officer and had once been arrested after being found in the grounds of Kensington Palace armed with two knives and a coil of rope. He had also served time in prison after being convicted of attempted rape. After being put under police surveillance for a few days, Barry was arrested on 25 May 2000 and charged a few days later.

The hard evidence against him was tiny. Nothing more than a speck, in fact: a solitary microscopic particle of firearm discharge residue that was found in the pocket of a coat at his home.

The only other evidence amounted to sightings of Barry loitering around the general area, anecdotal rumours of him having been seen following local women, and the fact that he had a smattering of newspaper articles about the murder in his flat — perhaps understandable, bearing in mind how close he lived to the victim.

At his trial the following year Barry was represented by the highly respected Michael Mansfield QC. Michael spent a lot of time exploring the Serbian hitman theory.

Before he knew where he was the focus of the jury's minds had shifted from 'Can the prosecution prove Barry George's guilt' to 'Who did it? Barry George or the Serbians?'. This meant that once the Crown had been able to cast enough doubt on the Serbian theory it left Barry alone in the jury's sights.

In his summing up the judge effectively directed the jury that unless they were sure that the particle of firearms discharge found on Barry's coat came from the same gun used to shoot Miss Dando there was no case for him to answer. But on 25 July 2001, Barry was convicted of murder by a 10-1 majority and sentenced to life in prison. Many people in the law were astonished by the verdict. Barry's defence team, led by Michael, later appealed against his conviction on the grounds that it was unsafe, but were unsuccessful.

However, it was clear that the reporting of the prosecution firearms expert's evidence at the trial had excited some comment in expert quarters. He had said that the discovery of the firearms discharge particle in Barry's coat made it more likely than not he was the killer, or had been in contact with the murder weapon. But other firearms experts who had read what he was reported to have said in the press asked 'How on earth can he have deduced that?' and went public with their concerns.

As the years passed, Barry continued to protest his innocence. Finally in 2006 his new lawyers, Carter Moore in Manchester, who specialise in miscarriages of justice, hired me to assist in asking the Criminal Cases Review Commission to refer the case back to the Court of Appeal. Normally once a defendant has lost an appeal against his conviction he cannot appeal for a second time. But it was recognised many years ago that this could result in miscarriages of justice not being corrected where, for example, fresh evidence came to light many years later and the Commission can send back a case to the Court of Appeal.

In June 2007, the Criminal Cases Review Commission did this for Barry's case. I appeared for him in the second appeal heard by three judges including the Lord Chief Justice, Lord Phillips of Worth Matravers.

Several witnesses, including the firearms expert who had given evidence for the prosecution at the Old Bailey, testified that the discovery of that one particle of residue in Barry's coat pocket was evidentially insignificant. They told the court that its presence did not make it more likely that he was the killer, or that he had been in contact with the gun used to kill her a year earlier, than if the particle had never been discovered in the first place, making it a completely neutral piece of evidence. Indeed during my cross-examination, the prosecution expert went so far as to concede that his evidence had been misrepresented at the Old Bailey.

After the Lord Chief Justice and his fellow judges had listened to our firearms experts it seemed fairly clear that no one could be sure the jury at the first trial would have reached a guilty verdict if it heard the correct evidence. The judges quashed Barry's conviction and ordered a retrial.

So it was that I found myself then defending a man who had at various times in his life believed himself to be Garry Glitter, a crack SAS soldier, a stuntman called Steve Majors and Freddie Mercury's cousin.

It promised to be a challenging case, for several reasons.

Barry wasn't the brightest of men and had a lot of difficulties coping in society. I sought the expert advice of Professor Michael Kopelman, a consultant psychiatrist at Kings College, London. Prof Kopelman did extensive tests on Barry and concluded that Barry had considerable mental issues and a limited ability to cope with the stresses and strains of ordinary life. His IQ was put at 75, placing him in the bottom 5% of the population.

When I looked at the photographs police had taken inside his flat following his arrest it was clear Barry was existing in a fairly desperate state. He had hoarded thousands of newspapers which were piled up all over the place. He didn't have a job and was living off benefits. His life seemed to involve little more than wandering the streets.

A rather pathetic character, he had a reputation for following attractive girls and making a bit of a nuisance of himself. In some ways his predicament reminded me of Colin Stagg's. Both men were loners who had been arrested more than a year after high-profile murders when — lacking any proper suspects — the police had been reduced to hauling in the local eccentrics.

My tactics for the retrial were different to those employed by Michael Mansfield seven years earlier. I wanted to put all the onus on the prosecution to prove my client had been responsible for Miss Dando's death. I refused to put up any distracting alternative scenarios suggesting who might have been responsible and would drive home my message that 'It wasn't Barry'. Ruling your client out as the killer is usually a far better course of action than trying to solve the crime yourself.

The particle of firearms discharge residue found inside the pocket of Barry's coat was the only hard bit of evidence against him. But had a police forensics team swept the clothes of the 12 jurors at his retrial they would almost certainly have found similar particles. The particles do not degrade. Once a firearm is discharged then the firearm discharge residue remains as a constant presence to be picked up moved about and attached to anyone who comes into contact with it. Every bus, every train and every underground station will contain such particles, in just the same way that almost every bank note in a person's wallet will have traces of cocaine. It doesn't mean that someone has been taking drugs any more than the presence of a particle of firearm discharge residue means they have been in contact with a firearm.

During the first trial the prosecution had argued that the presence of the firearm discharge residue, matching that which had been discharged when Ms Dando had been shot, found in the pocket of a coat recovered from

Barry George's flat made it was more likely that Barry had been in contact with the murder weapon than it was that the particle had been in his pocket by chance. In my view, this was an assumption which could not possibly be made in isolation without further supporting evidence.

During the first trial Michael had attempted to explain the presence of the particle by suggesting to the jury that it had come into contact with Barry's coat as a result of cross-contamination from the police or forensic scientists. When the prosecution were able to prove that there couldn't have been any such cross-contamination, Michael and his defence team were left with nowhere else to go. With the advantage of the fresh evidence I could take a different approach and concluded that the best way to win the retrial was to have the firearms discharge residue evidence ruled inadmissible by the judge.

But first I had to read through the case papers to identify any other cracks in the prosecution case. The material was mountainous: 24 lever arch files of evidence – the whole transcript of the first trial, all the experts' reports and all the statements gathered during the enormous police inquiry. Everything needed reading over and over again to make sure I didn't overlook anything that could be crucial to Barry's fate. It took weeks, while I was doing other cases. If I wasn't in court I might spend six hours a day reading, if I was in court, perhaps three hours.

I certainly couldn't fault the Metropolitan Police for effort. Detectives had followed up every possible avenue of investigation, but to very little effect.

In December 2007 Barry entered a not guilty plea when he reappeared at the Old Bailey and his retrial was fixed for June the following year. My problem was that I was getting married to my wife Gay on 28 June 2008, slap bang in the middle of the trial. There could be no question of postponing the trial because Barry had already spent eight years in prison. Fortunately, the prosecuting barrister, Jonathan Laidlaw QC, and his junior Duncan Penny, raised no objection to the court rising on a Thursday and sitting again on a Tuesday to allow the wedding to go ahead. Which shows how members of the Bar can behave kindly to each other even during hard-fought cases.

Before the jury had even been sworn in, I persuaded the judge, Mr Justice Griffiths-Williams, that the prosecution's firearms discharge particle evidence should be thrown out. Anybody could unwittingly pick up these minute particles of firearm discharge residue. But there were a number of other issues I still had to deal with.

Barry had mental capacity issues and during the trial we constantly needed to reassure him and to go over, sometimes endlessly, the points that he was anxious about. Indeed, if we hadn't seen him every evening after court I don't think he would have been able to cope with the proceedings the following morning. He was a very needy man, but my junior Jeff Samuels and I realised that unless we saw him every day – sometimes twice a day – he wouldn't survive the court session without exploding.

Fortunately, he never did. Somewhere in his psyche he knew that however much he wanted to give vent to his frustrations and feelings of injustice he shouldn't do so in court.

Also problematic was the evidence of a woman who claimed to have seen a man fitting Barry's description in Gowan Avenue at around the time Miss Dando was murdered. Barry's memory of his own movements was very uncertain, particularly so nine years later. So the question of whether it was Barry she had seen had featured very heavily in the first trial. There was no reason to believe for a moment that the woman was being untruthful or doing anything other than giving her best recollections of what she had seen. I had to spend quite a lot of time thinking about how I would deal with her evidence in court, because it was potentially damaging to the defence case. It didn't help that Barry, with all his inadequacies and faced with an allegation that he had committed an awful crime, had for years been trying to remember what he was doing at the time in question and ended up convincing himself he had a genuine memory of events that it is most unlikely he really had.

Aggressively cross-examining this witness would have been the wrong thing to do and would have run the risk of alienating myself in the eyes of the jury. A normal member of the public will not lie about such a matter. They may be right, they may be wrong, but they are not going to mislead the court deliberately. When you are cross-examining a witness who has an obvious motive for lying, perhaps to deflect blame for a crime onto someone else, you can go in hard and try to expose them. But this lady wasn't that kind of witness. I handled her delicately, gently calling her powers of recollection into question, and managed to create a doubt in the minds of the jurors as to the veracity of her evidence.

There were other witnesses who had helped the police establish some of Barry's movements that fateful day in April, 1999. Barry had visited a minicab office where he had spoken to several people. He had also been to a local charity, Hammersmith & Fulham Action on Disability, as well as a nearby health centre. But the police were unable to paint a clear picture of where he was at the time Miss Dando was murdered.

Three ladies at the charity all gave evidence saying that Barry called on them between 11.50am and 12 noon. I argued that if they were right it would have been impossible for him to have murdered Miss Dando at 11.30am and then gone home (walking in the opposite direction to the tall man seen leaving her house) to get changed before visiting the charity offices.

Our case was helped by the rejection of the prosecution's flimsy firearms evidence, the fact that two people who had almost certainly seen the killer moments after the murder took place later failed to pick Barry out at an identification parade, and the confusion surrounding his movements. On 1 August 2008, the jury foreman at the trial uttered the words: 'Not Guilty' and Barry's eight years in jail for Miss Dando's murder came to a juddering and final halt.

To this day I have no better idea than anyone else who killed Miss Dando but I am certain that it wasn't Barry George. It is dreadful that he had to spend so long locked up for a crime that he didn't commit. He received no compensation because he was unable to prove beyond reasonable doubt that he was innocent, which is the high test that is set before compensation is awarded. At least he was still alive.

CHAPTER TWENTY-TWO

Bribery and Corruption

~

Although most of my time is spent representing individuals, I also advise multinational companies on criminal law. While it is a somewhat strange concept, providing certain conditions are met, a company can be prosecuted and fined like any human defendant in the criminal courts.

Corporations approach me because they have been accused of committing crimes or wish to avoid committing crimes in the future. Over the past few years the bulk of this advice has concerned bribery and corruption. Although both occur in the United Kingdom, they pale into insignificance when set against the vast financial chicanery and feather-nesting in many other countries, especially in the developing world, and particularly in Africa and Asia. In the mid-20th Century any British company that wanted to do business overseas in certain states was almost certain to encounter corrupt individuals, organisations and even governments. Multimillion-pound development projects frequently came to a halt because of mysterious last-minute 'technical issues' that could only be resolved by the payment of a specified sum of money. Faced with the prospect of losing everything they had invested in money, manpower and effort, many UK companies parted with large sums of money to 'unlock' the barriers erected by traders and officials.

Such corruption took many forms. Sometimes the British company did not pay the bribe that landed a contract. Instead, the payment was made by an overseas consultant hired by the firm to resolve any problems. Traditionally when British companies, reluctantly in my experience, engaged in bribery, they did so in the belief that they couldn't be prosecuted back home for payments made abroad.

Jurisdiction in criminal cases was, historically, considered to be teritorial. If you bribed someone in Delhi, it was a crime only in Delhi. However if part of the offence took place in this country, with perhaps the payment being made from here, then jurisdiction could flow from that.

All that changed when Britain signed an international anti-bribery convention drafted by the Organisation for Economic Co-Operation and Development (OECD). The 2010 Bribery Act, which enshrined the convention in UK law, clarified the law and made it clear that British companies were liable to prosecution if they paid or received bribes abroad. As well as creating a number of new offences, it turned out to be a bonanza for barristers' chambers in London. The Bribery Act was not retrospective, so there was no risk of companies being prosecuted under the Act for alleged wrongdoing in the past. But a lot of blue chip companies — household names in Britain — approached me and other barristers asking how they should behave in the future. Hypothetically, they would say: 'This is how we used to do things. Can we still do them like this or might we now be prosecuted under anti-bribery legislation?'

While unable to divulge the specifics of the cases, the details made for fascinating reading. For a start money is not usually demanded blatantly as a bribe, it is disguised in many ways, for example the overpayment for goods supplied locally, or a requirement to source catering from a particular company which just happens to charge 10 times the market rate. In the past, a condition of a big building contract might have been that a local architect had to sign off on the building before stage payments were made. This is quite standard in many industries all around the world, but in Africa the local architect might suddenly say: 'I'm sorry I can't possibly sign that off' and make some entirely spurious excuse as to why he couldn't. In such a case the only way he would approve the instalment would be if he were given a contract by that same company to do some work on another, entirely fictitious project — in other words, a bribe.

My confidential advice has been varied, covering British companies trading all over Africa and Asia, on contracts for commodities, motor vehicle parts, the building of bridges, dams and railway lines, the renewal of railway stock and the shipment of oil. I advised one well-known oil company whether paying certain taxes to an illegal regime could amount to supporting terrorism. Such situations occasionally arise when a government has lost control and a country has fragmented into different parts, or where an armed rebel group makes a Unilateral Declaration of Independence, such as within a country like Libya or Iraq.

I might very well advise a company that their previous way of doing business was not unlawful under the old law or the new, or alternatively I might advise that to continue to trade in the way they have in the past might breach the Bribery Act. Whichever it was, I would give them my expert legal advice in an 'opinion' — a short written report by a barrister containing his opinion on the question for which his advice is sought.

Sometimes tens of millions of pounds could turn on the advice given and that is when we barristers are grateful that our professional overseeers require us to take out indemnity insurance in case we act negligently in giving such advice. Fortunately, so far, no-one has sought to sue me for giving advice that was later found to be wrong.

In my experience companies are, by and large, very anxious not to commit crime. Sadly, those that behave honestly by blowing the whistle on corruption discovered internally sometimes end up losing out financially. Self-reporting that you've done something wrong is no guarantee that you won't be prosecuted. It isn't always possible to cut a deal with the Serious Fraud Office, but a company can only be prosecuted if one of its controlling minds knew what was going on. A controlling mind of a company is someone, normally a director, who actually controlled the actions of the company in a material way. Controlling minds are easy to identify in a small company, but harder to identify in larger ones.

My advice is usually that failing to self-report carries with it a risk that is just not worth taking. All companies are audited and payments without a proper audit trail invite being uncovered. In today's fast-moving world of social media, businesses must also bear in mind the reputational damage that tends to follow any attempt to cover up wrongdoing.

Now most countries enforce the anti-bribery legislation strictly. More than 40 countries worldwide have signed up to the OECD convention and British companies are still liable to prosecution if they have bribed a public official anywhere in the world, regardless of whether or not they are signatories to the convention. In my view, the OECD's anti-bribery convention and the domestic legislation that has followed it have done a great deal to stamp out corruption around the world, although there are still some countries where bribery is deeply entrenched.

Lucrative, high-stakes takeovers can also be another area where the advice of barristers is sought. When one company takes over another, the company that is being taken over is obliged to give a fair account of its assets and liabilities and to disclose anything that might affect its value. There should be no skeletons in the boardroom cupboard.

When a takeover is referred to the Competition and Markets Authority (formerly the Competition Commission and before that the Monopolies and Mergers Commission) there is a delay before the market is informed whether the takeover will proceed. During that delay neither side is permitted to pull out of the deal, unless some material undisclosed fact is discovered while the panel decide whether the takeover can proceed. I've known the company mounting a takeover to discover something that hasn't been disclosed by its intended target which has caused it to change its mind with the result that it will try to rely upon the recent undisclosed facts to justify them pulling out of the takeover.

In those situations I've been asked to say whether some previously undisclosed fact, possibly a bribery allegation in a country where the company operates, would be material and constitute a legal basis for pulling out of the takeover. In such cases I've known silks to be engaged by both companies involved and a third silk by the Panel.

I also advised the Liberal Democrats after its former chief executive, Lord Rennard, was accused of sexually harassing female party workers. The party wanted to know if it could publish the results of an independent inquiry into how the allegations had been dealt with internally while the police carried out a criminal investigation, in case it risked prejudicing any potential trial. My advice was that the party could publish *Report into the Processes and Culture within The Liberal Democrat Party*, because it wouldn't impact on any future criminal case. It was most unlikely any juror would read it, and even if they did it would be perfectly reasonable to ask them to put it out of their mind for the purposes of making sure only evidence presented at trial was taken into consideration. My advice was 'publish and be damned' — and the Liberal Democrats did. There was a police investigation, but the Crown Prosecution Service decided there was insufficient evidence to bring any charges, so there never was a trial.

Much of the advice we give as barristers is confidential and the situations we are asked to advise upon never become public. Our clients are entitled to have their affairs dealt with confidentially and hence much of what we do cannot be written about until or unless it has already been made public.

CHAPTER TWENTY-THREE

Case 12
A Ghetto Shoot-out in Jamaica

~

I walked through the security cordon into Downing Street, past the Prime Minister's home at No 10, and entered No 12. I was in an ornate, wood-panelled room; but the bloody event to which my mind was turning had taken place five years previously in Kingston, Jamaica.

I had spent several days preparing for the case of Marlon Moodie and what I would have to say on 9 July 2003 would decide whether he was sentenced to hang. I very much hoped I would succeed. I imagine he did, too, though I never spoke to him.

How I came to be arguing for a defendant's life – rather than his liberty – had its roots deep in the British Empire. Once an assembly of the Queen's advisors, Her Majesty's

Most Honourable Privy Council heard all appeals from Britain's colonies including Australia, India and Canada. On gaining independence most of these states established their own Supreme Court and dispensed with the Privy Council in London. A few small territories, however — the British Overseas Territories, the Crown Dependencies, and some ex-colonies in the West Indies — kept the Privy Council as their final Court of Appeal.

Many defendants from the West Indies cannot afford to hire a legal team costing thousands of pounds a day to argue their case in the Privy Council Chamber — even if their life is at stake. So, solicitors and barristers offer their services for free or *pro bono* (*pro bono publico* in Latin: for the public good) in Privy Council cases from the West Indies. Allocated under a rota system called the 'London List', a solicitor calls up and says: 'We've got a case and we'd like Mr Clegg to do it.'

It's instilled into barristers that we must put something back into the profession, so when the case of Marlon Moodie and his alleged accomplice Andrew Hunter came through I was always going to take it. All I was focused on was making sure we won.

Moodie and Hunter were gunmen, gangsters perhaps, in Kingston in the years when drug gangs ruled the ghettos of Jamaica's capital, and they had been convicted of murdering a policeman. Hunter had been spared the death penalty because he was under 18, but Moodie was of age and was sentenced to hang. The Court of Appeal of Jamaica had rejected the men's appeal against their convictions in October 2001. Although there was a temporary stay on the death penalty in Jamaica, the risk was that the moratorium would be lifted and Moodie would be executed.

On receiving the case papers, I spent several days carefully combing through the transcript of the trial and the subsequent appeal. I never saw or spoke to Moodie or Hunter because they were in prison in Jamaica and I was in London; there were no video conference facilities available that we could use. At any rate, the case was about the law rather than the facts, so there wasn't much point.

The case papers brought alive the events of 5 November 1998, in the violent Dunkirk area of Kingston, Jamaica's capital. Four members of the Jamaica Constabulary Force had been inside an unmarked police car as it had trundled along Wild Street. As they passed a shop they saw two individuals known to them: Hunter and Moodie, who were quickly joined by two others, Stammer and Foreigner. Together the men pulled guns from their waist and fired at the police car.

The officers, armed with 9mm semi-automatic pistols, got out of the car to return fire and the gunmen fled. One constable stayed with the police car, while the others split up. Constables Phillip Mitchell and Orlando Milton headed down William Street, while Constable Dewar — in what was to be a fateful decision — headed down Shoe Lane.

Police saw Hunter and Moodie firing on Constable

Dewar, who was hit and fell down. He was pronounced dead at hospital. The question for the courts over the ensuing years was: who had shot him?

Constable Dewar had been shot by several bullets, most of which had passed through his body and were not recovered but a bullet taken from his chest was from something like a .45 calibre pistol. Forensic evidence was unable to be more exact. A police officer at the scene found a single expended .45 cartridge and five 9mm shells lying nearby on the ground.

A search of the area later yielded Hunter and Moodie and they were taken for questioning. Each blamed someone else for firing at Constable Dewar. Hunter told the interviewing superintendent: 'Mr Robinson, me nuh fire no shot. A Marlon fire de shot.' Moodie told the superintendent: 'Mr Robinson, you know say a Stammer kill the police. Mi nuh fire nuh shot.'

At their trial, both Hunter and Moodie flatly denied that they were present at the scene.

In her summing up, the judge, Mrs Justice Smith, explained the law of joint enterprise, where one gang member can be found guilty of an act committed by another gang member. She told the jury:

> Let me just tell you that where two persons embark on a joint enterprise, each is liable for the act done in pursuance of that joint enterprise. If you should find that one kills and this was in pursuance of this common design, then

> both would be guilty. In other words, the one who didn't fire the firearm could not come and say: "No, I didn't fire".

In Jamaica the sentence for murder is normally life in jail but killing a police officer doing his duty is capital murder, punishable by death. In order to be convicted of capital murder, a defendant must have been the one who actually killed the murder victim, the 'triggerman'. It is not enough just to have been part of a joint enterprise.

Mrs Justice Smith instructed the jury to return verdicts on capital murder, the death penalty offence. On 22 March 2000, the jury found both the men guilty and Moodie was sentenced to hang.

Was that right? Three years later the case was heard by the Privy Council, sitting 7,500 miles away. At the time the judicial committee of the Privy Council sat in a special court in Downing Street[6]. I presented the case from a wooden lectern rather like a cage in the middle of the room. The five judges sat in front of me without wigs or robes, wearing business suits. One was wearing a white linen jacket.

A simple majority of three or more judges could decide the case. In the past one or two judges were thought to oppose the death penalty so vehemently that they would look sympathetically upon any conceivable error that would allow them to commute a death sentence but I

6 Since 2009 it has been based in the Supreme Court building opposite the Houses of Parliament

didn't feel any particular support when I began to present my case. My arguments had to pass muster.

Setting out my case, mindful of its consequences, I argued that Mrs Justice Smith was wrong to restrict the jury to returning verdicts on capital murder only.

Firstly, I argued, the judge had confused the jury by mentioning joint enterprise when that law could never apply to a case of capital murder. Jurors might have been given the impression that it did not matter which gunman had pulled the trigger.

Secondly, and more importantly, the police evidence that both Hunter and Moodie fired at Constable Dewar had been contradicted:

- Firstly, in their police interviews each man had blamed another for firing the fatal shot. (Although the defendants chose not to rely on these statements, I pointed out that the judge could have considered them when deciding what verdict the jury could return).
- Secondly, two other known gunmen — Stammer and Foreigner — were in the vicinity of the shooting.
- Thirdly, regardless of whether Hunter or Moodie, or both, had fired their guns, the ballistic evidence did not show decisively that Constable Dewar had been killed by more than one bullet. He may have survived some of his injuries, thus it was perfectly possible that only one of the defendants had fired the fatal shot.

Three months later the judges unanimously ruled that by discussing the law of joint enterprise before allowing only capital murder, Judge Smith had confused the jury.

They agreed that she should also have stressed the importance of the 'triggerman' test — who had fired the fatal shot or shots at Constable Dewar — and allowed verdicts of capital or non-capital murder.

The judges substituted verdicts of non-capital murder for capital murder. Regardless of whether the temporary ban on executions was lifted, Moodie would never hang.

Most barristers share my abhorrence towards capital punishment, not least because the wrong person can be convicted, as happened with Barry George for the murder of Jill Dando. So my commitment was deeper than just securing a victory. While this appeal wasn't the most interesting legally, the outcome mattered more than any other case I have fought.

Afterwards Marlon Moodie sent me a letter of thanks, albeit a moving one, in broken English.

I didn't keep it. I hardly keep any letters I'm sent. I'm not sentimental; remaining detached helps me stay focussed on the law. Once I have finished a case and the immediate euphoria wears off, it becomes marked 'old' in my mind. I erase it and make space for the next one.

CHAPTER TWENTY-FOUR

Trying Times for Legal Aid

~

Legal Aid. Two little words seem to set hackles rising everywhere, whether in a newspaper editor's office or the local pub. Everyone seems to have a view on the public funding of defence fees, and it's invariably a negative one, but the simple fact of the matter is that without Legal Aid we could not even begin to pretend we have a proper criminal justice system.

If you believe, as I do, that everyone is entitled to a fair trial, it follows that every individual must have access to proper legal representation regardless of their financial status. Legal Aid was designed precisely to do just that, by paying for an appropriate defence for those with limited means.

For decades the system worked well: courts were fully staffed, the Crown Prosecution Service budget was adequate and Legal Aid defendants were represented properly. The barristers defending them earned a fee that was independently assessed to be fair and reasonable. This is no longer the case.

The criminal justice system has been battered by a decade of government cuts. Barristers (along with solicitors) have borne the brunt. To be blunt I think lawyers have fallen out of favour with the Treasury. The Treasury hated the fact that there is no cap to the Legal Aid budget. Every normal government department is given 'x' millions of pounds to spend annually, but Legal Aid is unlimited, because once you have offered everyone arrested legal representation you must meet that promise. The more people you arrest the more you must pay.

The number of criminal cases has actually fallen, by 6% between 2010 and 2017, but those that reach court are often more complex and consequently require more time. The Serious Fraud Office, for instance, prosecutes frauds that wouldn't have been prosecuted 30 years ago, because it now has the expertise and funds necessary to launch proceedings. There are also many more cases of historic sexual abuse going through the courts.

Considering these two trends, one would have expected spending on the criminal justice system to have stayed broadly the same, if not to have risen in line with inflation. Instead, swingeing cuts have been made to Legal Aid, as well as to the Crown Prosecution Service and H.M. Courts & Tribunal Service. Between 2010-11 and 2017-18, the budget of the Ministry of Justice, which funds them, was cut more than any other government department, from £8.7bn to £6.6 billion. It must lop off a further £600 million by 2019-20.

Court staffing has been reduced. In most court centres there are not enough clerks or ushers for each courtroom and they have to run two courts at the same time. The result is that often a judge cannot sit because no staff are available and they must wait until someone is released by another court. So time and efficiency is lost.

The budget for maintaining the courts has fallen. Stories of leaking roofs, toilets that do not flush, lifts that do not work and heating and air conditioning systems that are broken are commonplace. The courts themselves have not been painted in years, carpets are threadbare and there is a general feeling of squalor that you might expect in a developing country (but curiously do not find there, because respect for the rule of law demands that courts are properly maintained). Here, in one of the largest economies in Europe, that does not appear to be the case.

How else to describe the especially deep cuts to public representation? Between 2005-6 and 2015-16 the Legal Aid budget was slashed by more than 40%, from £2.6bn to £1.5bn. While every defendant charged with a criminal offence in the Crown Court may claim Legal Aid (assuming they are not wealthy), the rates paid to barristers for defending them have plunged.

Take the fee for a plea of mitigation, which usually

takes place weeks after a defendant has been convicted. These hearings take place up and down the country every day. The barrister will have to read all the reports that have been sent to the court, perhaps read some references from employers and family and prepare the oral plea of mitigation to present to the court. They will have to travel to court, have a conference with the defendant and take him through the reports and advise on likely sentence, present the mitigation and then advise on any possible appeal. This process can frequently take an entire day, at the very least half a day. The payment for this is a standard fee of £87, working out at perhaps £10 an hour, maybe a little more and maybe a little less. This is less than a plumber or electrician (I don't want to imply that these trades are overpaid, I am just using them as an example.)

The impact of these rate cuts can be seen on the budgets of the three separate schemes which pay Legal Aid fees to barristers. Spending on the biggest, the Advocates Graduated Fee Scheme, fell from £362 million in 2005-6 to £226 million in 2016-17. Payments for graver crimes, under the Very High Cost Case scheme, shrank from £95 million 2009-10 to £31 million in 2016-17. Finally, over the same period recompense for wasted preparation has shrunk from £14 million to £3 million.

Because the costs of maintaining an office and staff have stayed the same, chambers have laid off staff, merged to reduce costs, or gone out of business. The take-home pay of the average barrister has halved. The average income of a barrister doing Legal Aid crime is now estimated to be £54,000 gross including VAT, which works out at approximately £28,000 a year net after expenses. This modest figure does not include any provision for sick pay, holiday pay, maternity or paternity pay, or a pension. A recent survey of young Legal Aid lawyers qualified for up to 10 years found that 30% were earning less than £20,000 and 53% less than £25,000.

It is no exaggeration to say that the profession is in crisis. We are rapidly approaching the position where only someone with a private income can afford to practice as a Legal Aid barrister, with the inevitable loss to diversity. It is no surprise that applications for pupillage in my chambers have fallen by a third in the past eight years.

Our chambers have been less affected than most because a few years ago we made a conscious decision to reduce our dependency on publicly-funded work. Fifteen years ago about 90% of our turnover came from Legal Aid, now it's about a third. Instead we encourage work from clients who can pay privately. Some are wealthy; others take out bank loans or a second mortgage on their home, or a trade union, local authority or legal insurer pays their fees. In effect, these private cases subsidise the Legal Aid ones. If we were all doing Legal Aid work we couldn't afford to stay at 2 Bedford Row. The drop in overall income would make it wholly uneconomic. And we would have to cut back on the pupillage awards we give to the best young lawyers.

The cuts in the Legal Aid budget have shaken the 'cab rank principle'. Previously the assumption was that a Legal Aid fee was reasonable and therefore a barrister had to accept a Legal Aid brief if offered one. Now, because the cuts have been so great, a barrister is entitled to say that they will not accept a Legal Aid case because the fee is not reasonable. So steep has been the reduction in rates that, regrettably, I and some colleagues at 2BR will no longer accept Legal Aid work.

One reason I won't take on new public-funded cases is that the service I could offer would be sub-standard. I would not be able to instruct the experts I have been instructing for years, because Legal Aid would not pay for them, and I would be faced with going to cheaper counterparts who I had less confidence in. I could not expect solicitors to do the volume of work I demand if they were not being paid properly for their time. What would be the point in taking on a case in those circumstances? I would just end up losing in court and failing my client.

Take the case of Barry George. He was legally aided in both his trials. When I represented Barry at his re-trial the cuts had started to bite and I received roughly half what Michael Mansfield was paid for defending him the first time. Nowadays I would have been paid about half again. Luckily, the experts had already committed to that case and a number of them had worked with me in the past; I could lean on them to help. But if Barry's solicitors had come to me now I would not be prepared to act in his case;

the experts that I instructed would likewise refuse to act. If Barry George were re-tried now, would justice be done? Would he have been able to prove the gunshot residue was irrelevant? Would he have been found not guilty?

Would he still be waking up every morning in a small cell, imprisoned year after year for a crime he did not commit?

The truth is that the years of savage cuts to the Legal Aid budget, the courts and the Crown Prosecution Service have badly damaged our system of criminal justice. They will lead to innocent people being convicted of crimes they did not commit and the guilty going free.

My personal perception is that the government doesn't really care whether people are well represented. It wants to ensure adequate representation so that it can't be hauled before the European Court of Human Rights by people complaining that they've been denied a fair trial, but it doesn't want to pay for strong defences, because, in its eyes, defendants are just a bunch of criminals — which makes a mockery of the principle that people are innocent until proven guilty.

The solution would be to devise a Legal Aid system that recognises the distinction between very serious crimes like murder and rape, and less serious crimes like assault and theft, and provides reasonable remuneration in each case, taking into account the responsibility the barrister has in the case and the work demanded from him. It cannot be done without a significant increase in the Legal Aid budget, which ought to be looked at not so much as an increase in funding but as the reinstatement of funding wrongly removed. Lawyers doing Legal Aid ought to be paid a reasonable fee. Reverting back to the Legal Aid pay rates of a decade ago would be a start.

CHAPTER TWENTY-FIVE

Case 13
The Murder of Joanna Yeates

~

That familiar question 'how can you represent them?' was asked of me with particular force after the murder of Joanna Yeates. Miss Yeates was a 25-year-old landscape gardener with everything to live for. She and her boyfriend Greg Reardon shared a flat in an imposing Victorian house in Canynge Road in the Clifton area of Bristol. Her disappearance at Christmas 2010 mystified her friends and family.

On 17 December, Miss Yeates had spent the evening drinking with colleagues in the Bristol Ram pub, confiding to some that she wasn't looking forward to the weekend, because Mr Reardon had gone to visit his brother in Sheffield. At around 8pm she set off on the half-hour walk to Clifton. She phoned a friend to arrange a drink on

Christmas Eve, then bought a pizza at a Tesco Express and two bottles of cider at an off-licence on her way home.

By the time Mr Reardon returned to their flat on 19 December, he was already worried: Miss Yeates had not been responding to his texts and calls. When she was nowhere to be seen, he became frantic. He called her mobile once more only to hear it ring in the pocket of her coat a few feet away. He quickly found her purse and keys and noticed that their cat didn't seem to have been fed. The 999 call he made just moments later to report her missing triggered one of the biggest police investigations in Bristol's history, Operation Braid.

Detectives spoke to several witnesses, including the local vicar, who said that they had seen Miss Yeates walking home alone. They had also found the two bottles of cider in the flat, one of which had been partially drunk.

In the run-up to Christmas, Miss Yeates's parents made several televised appeals for information, with her father David saying he feared she had been abducted because she would never have gone out leaving her keys and phone at home. Like millions of other people I had been following the rolling TV news coverage of the story. Its sad denouement came on Christmas Day: a couple out walking their dog discovered a body dumped in the snow near the entrance to a quarry three miles away in Failand, Somerset. Miss Yeates had been strangled. There appeared to be no obvious motive for her murder.

Police attention focussed on the area immediately

around Miss Yeates's flat. Detectives arrested her landlord, Christopher Jefferies, who lived in another flat in the same house. To my mind, it seemed that he had come under suspicion simply because of his unconventional dress sense and hairstyle. It was one of those classic, all-too-familiar murder cases where, in the absence of an obvious motive or any strong evidence pointing towards a suspect, the police had directed their investigatory efforts towards a local eccentric. Thankfully they soon realised they didn't even have a shred of evidence against Mr Jefferies and let him go. He was later proved to be completely innocent and successfully sued newspapers for defaming his character.

The police's gaze then fell upon another suspect. Like Miss Yeates's landlord, Vincent Tabak lived in another of the self-contained flats inside the large shared house where they were all resident. There was no evidence to suggest that Tabak and Miss Yeates knew each other beyond sharing the most casual of nods as passing neighbours. Tabak was 33, of good character, in a stable relationship, and had a good job in computers.

As well as living in the same building as Joanne, however, he was known to have been there at the time of her disappearance, on his own, since his girlfriend was elsewhere for Christmas. Footage from CCTV cameras showed Tabak's car visiting a supermarket late on 17 December. He was obviously out and about around the time she went missing. Could her body have been in his boot?

By the time the police's attention eventually turned

to Tabak he had already left Bristol to visit his family in Holland for New Year and the police needed a reason to travel across the Channel to see him. As it happened, Tabak himself provided them with one. While in Holland he tried to shift the focus of the police inquiry back on to Mr Jefferies and called the murder team claiming to have seen his neighbour using his car on the night Miss Yeates disappeared. The overly enthusiastic way in which he agreed to meet police at Amsterdam's Schiphol Airport to go over, once again, his whereabouts, and the circumstances surrounding Miss Yeates's disappearance and murder heightened suspicions. These intensified further when the police officer sent to take a statement from him noticed inconsistencies with his original story.

Tabak quickly became the prime suspect and he was arrested on 20 January 2011. When his car was seized traces of Miss Yeates's blood and DNA were found in the boot. His DNA was also found on her body. He was charged with murder.

Tabak initially claimed the DNA evidence against him had been fabricated by corrupt police officers who wanted to frame him. A month after his arrest, however, while on remand at Long Lartin Prison in Worcestershire, he confided to a chaplain that he had killed Miss Yeates but said that her death had been an accident.

Tabak was being represented by Kelsey & Hall, whose senior partner Ian Kelsey, a well-known solicitor in the West Country, also knew one of the barristers in my chambers, Dean Armstrong. Since I had done some high-profile murder cases, I was engaged to act for Tabak, with Dean as my junior. It was a classic example of a provincial law firm engaging the services of a London chambers because of a strong working relationship in the past.

In my meetings with him, Tabak was extremely courteous, almost deferential. He was bilingual and very bright. He had an excellent university degree and a good job at an engineering consultancy in Bristol. He spoke better English than most of my English clients. He readily understood the advice I gave him, and never needed anything explaining to him twice. He understood the court process and the relevant issues. It was unusual to have such an intelligent defendant charged with murder.

By the time I saw him for the first time he had already admitted he had committed the physical act of killing Miss Yeates, so there was no question of having to point out the strength of the evidence against him. He was prepared to plead guilty to manslaughter on the basis that he did not intend to kill Miss Yeates or cause her grievous bodily harm, the states of mind necessary to prove the offence of murder.

According to Tabak, he was leaving the house where he and Miss Yeates lived on the night of 17 December when he saw her through the kitchen window of her flat. She gestured to him that he should come in and have a Christmas drink, so he turned around and went back. Once inside her flat, he interpreted her actions as an invitation to make a pass at her and went to kiss her, but to his surprise she screamed. Panicking, he grabbed her around the throat with one of his hands to calm her down without intending to cause her any harm, but to his shock and disbelief, she died.

Tabak said all this happened within about 20 seconds. Doctors acknowledge that it is possible to kill someone quickly by applying pressure to the vagal nerve, which runs inside the jugular from the head down the throat towards the heart. The special forces use the technique to kill people.

Tabak's manslaughter plea wasn't accepted by the Crown Prosecution Service and in May 2011 his case was sent for trial at Bristol Crown Court.

At the pre-trial hearings, which as usual were subject to reporting restrictions to prevent the jury being prejudiced, I asked the judge to rule some evidence about Tabak's behaviour inadmissible. Tabak had a very extensive collection of extreme and violent pornography which the prosecution said was relevant because it showed women being held by the neck in a way that must have been similar to what happened to Miss Yeates. The prosecution maintained that he had strangled her for sexual gratification, but this was purely theoretical. There was nothing in his past to indicate any predilection for that sort of conduct. He had no criminal record at all. I managed to persuade the trial judge, Mr Justice Field, to exclude all the evidence of the pornography. The prosecution also wanted to put in evidence the fact that Tabak had contacted prostitutes in the United States when on a visit there but I got that ruled inadmissible too.

I was less successful with another pre-trial challenge. Tabak had also done a lot of internet research between the killing and his arrest, regarding the length of time it takes a body to decompose and the offence of manslaughter. I was unable to get that thrown out. I was able to argue in court, however, that this research wasn't as damning as it might appear because Tabak knew he'd killed Miss Yeates and had later admitted doing so. His explanation for the events of that night was still feasible.

At his trial, which began in October 2011, a lot of time was spent exploring Tabak's timings. He stated that he had chatted to Miss Yeates before things suddenly went wrong, while the prosecution maintained that she must have been killed virtually the moment she got home. The Crown was able to plot her journey pretty accurately using CCTV evidence gathered by the police and the testimony of witnesses. The forensic evidence indicated she had died in her own kitchen, but that at some point before dumping her body Tabak had taken Miss Yeates back to his own flat. The television had also been left on in her flat, indicating she was in the midst of ordinary life when she was interrupted. There was no sign of him having broken in. It is unclear if she had beckoned him in as he claimed, or whether he had rung her door bell.

The prosecution asserted that Miss Yeates hadn't been

home long enough for Tabak's account to be truthful. Some people arriving at a party being thrown at a house on the other side of the road claimed to have heard a scream soon after she would have got home. The police believed this was Miss Yeates screaming as she was being attacked, but I suspected the two properties were so far away and the walls of Miss Yeates's flat so thick that the sound would not have carried.

As usual, I went to the property where the partygoers claimed to have heard the scream while a colleague, accompanied by the police, went to the victim's flat and screamed. It was very difficult to hear anything on a quiet afternoon. On the evening that Miss Yeates was killed there were various parties in the area as it was the last day of the university term. Nobody dialled 999 at the time so it was safe to assume that nobody heard anything that they interpreted at the time as a scream from someone being attacked. During the trial the jury visited the scene, too, and they were able to decide whether whatever the partygoers had heard was likely to have come from Miss Yeates's flat.

Much turned on how long it would take for someone to die if the vagal nerve was gripped. I called Dr Nat Cary, a respected pathologist, who explained that it was possible to kill someone in less than five seconds if you put your hand around their throat in a particular way. The prosecution pathologist said it probably took between 15 and 30 seconds. The quicker Miss Yeates's death the more feasible Tabak's lack of intent was. But even if the jury accepted the evidence of our renowned expert over the prosecution's it was still possible that Tabak had intended to commit murder.

It didn't help his case that the trial heard a lot of evidence about how he behaved after Miss Yeates's death — when he attended dinner parties, where he was unsurprisingly asked about the killing. Several guests thought he behaved oddly at those dinner parties but that was with the benefit of hindsight.

Sometimes in a murder case I advise a client not to give evidence. Tabak could have chosen to stay silent, but that was not a sensible option in his situation. He didn't need persuading to give evidence. I went over his account with him time and time again. A barrister can't rehearse a witness but we can discuss the evidence with them and ask their explanation for certain things. Tabak's explanation for not immediately calling an ambulance after Miss Yeates collapsed was simply that he had panicked.

He was on the witness stand for days. I didn't hit him with the classic opening gambit 'Did you mean to kill her?' Instead I tried to humanise him in front of the jury. I had to get him to describe how the killing actually took place, but I left the key question until later in his evidence. I asked: 'Did you intend to kill Miss Yeates? Did you intend to cause her really serious bodily harm?' He replied: 'No,' in a rather matter of fact but not sterile way.

The prosecutor, Nigel Lickley QC, leader of the Western Circuit, was thorough in his cross-examination, focusing on the time it would take in anyone's view for someone to die in those circumstances and what Tabak had been thinking at the time.

Bearing in mind the obvious difficulties in his case, I think Tabak gave quite compelling evidence. Nobody could say his explanation for Miss Yeates's death was impossible. I have conducted slenderer defences. The question was whether the jury believed him.

They were out for nearly three days before returning their verdict. Tabak was convicted of murder on a 10-2 majority. Two of the jurors clearly believed him, or at any rate weren't certain of his guilt. One more uncertain juror would have forced a retrial. Looking back there certainly wasn't a seminal moment where the defence case fell apart because of an unexpected development, which I've known in the past.

It wasn't a rare defeat. I have lost plenty of the 100-plus murder trials I've done over the years. Defence barristers are used to losing. Statistically, more prosecutions result in conviction than acquittal and that has always been the case. However, I have won more murder trials than I've lost (it's probably 60-40 in favour of acquittals). In any case, having a jury return a verdict of manslaughter rather than murder is regarded as a victory, though that wasn't the case here.

To this day nobody really knows why Tabak killed Miss Yeates. Aside from Vincent Tabak, that is.

CHAPTER TWENTY-SIX

Private Clients

~

Generally I act for defendants who have been accused of a crime. Sometimes, however, I am engaged to represent a suspect — usually a wealthy private client — before any charges have been brought. What I'm really being asked to do at this stage is to advise the defendant during the course of a police investigation.

At this stage there may not be many papers to read. The prosecution may have disclosed some material, though it's often sparse, and my client may have relevant documents too. At a conference we will discuss the kind of questions they may be asked in a police interview, explore whether they have any paperwork supporting their innocence that could be disclosed to the police and possibly take helpful statements from family members, friends or business associates.

If I feel that the police case is weak I may make representations to the Crown Prosecution Service arguing that the evidence against my client, as disclosed to me, does not meet the threshold required for charging. If I am successful, then I will not expect to see that client again. This happened recently with a solicitor who was suspected of trying to pervert the course of justice by putting his wife down as the driver of a car when it was caught speeding by some camera. Needless to say, it was an honest mistake, so I put forward a written representation as to how the mistake came to be made. In that case no charges were brought. Whether that was as a result of my representation or whether the CPS would have come to that decision anyway, I don't know.

In another case a schoolmaster was accused of indecency with a child. Again, I made representations about salient facts from the case: that the child's account was inconsistent, that the child was having lots of problems at school, that the child was known to fantasise as shown in the school records, and that the events were almost impossible to have unfolded as alleged, because other children would have seen what had happened. I argued that the charge should never have been brought because of the frailties in the prosecution case. In this case I didn't succeed and the schoolmaster was charged. He was found not guilty by a jury after about 10 minutes of retirement. The judge in that case ordered the CPS to pay all the costs of the defence, pointing out in part that the case should never have been brought and they ought perhaps to have listened to the representations they received.

Obviously in those situations I would stand to earn more money if my client was charged, but it would never cross my mind to string out a case or to avoid making advance submissions in order to generate a higher fee. In any event I would never get away with it because other people – not least my instructing solicitor and my professional colleagues – would realise something was amiss. Although barristers don't swear an oath like the physician's Hippocratic Oath, when we are called to the Bar and accept our copy of *Duty and Art in Advocacy* we tacitly agree to abide by the ethics of our profession which are about doing the best for our clients. Barristers should never allow personal financial advantage to influence the way we represent someone and in my 40-odd years at the Bar I have never known one to act to the contrary.

In other cases I will be instructed after the case has already been sent for trial, which means I will have a lot of preparation to do. Where there are multiple defendants this can mean an enormous amount of reading. In some big fraud trials I have had to wade through tens of thousands of documents disclosed by the Serious Fraud Office. This has often included the entirety of the evidence against every defendant, not just mine.

Good barristers can quickly read files and identify what is important within them. (Speed reading is a difficult habit to break, and I find it hard to read a newspaper properly.)

Obviously some bits of information require more detailed scrutiny than others. I will often come across a section of evidence which I recognise as being especially important and spend many hours reading, re-reading and cross-referencing it. Sometimes, when reading case papers for the first time, I may spot something that appears to me to be of obvious importance but which has somehow escaped the attention of my instructing solicitors or a previous legal team. That is not a criticism of anybody. Sometimes it's possible to get swamped by paperwork. But a fresh pair of eyes cast over the same material will often unearth something that has been missed previously.

One of my recent cases involved representing a medical student in Gloucester Magistrates Court who was accused of making an obscene hand gesture to a neighbour with his fist. The student's solicitors had amassed a welter of evidence to put before the magistrates court regarding where the neighbour was standing when the gesture was allegedly made and whether he could possibly have seen any such gesture. Nobody, though, appeared to have questioned whether or not by simply moving your hand you could actually be guilty of a criminal offence.

When I met the young man and his solicitors for the first time at a case conference I said: 'Hang on, this is ridiculous, how can this be a crime?' It seemed to me that it would be impossible for the prosecution to prove beyond reasonable doubt that by moving his fist up and down the defendant deliberately intended to cause offence and was guilty of obscene behaviour.

By the time the case came around and I finally got to stand up in court and address the magistrates I suggested that if making such a gesture amounted to a criminal offence the police would have to arrest half the people attending football matches up and down the country every Saturday. Luckily for the young man in question the magistrates took my point on board and he was acquitted. The case had lasted for six whole months before anybody had the temerity to question its foundation.

It was a classic case of people not being able to see the wood for the trees.

CHAPTER TWENTY-SEVEN

Case 14
The Phone Hacking Trial

~

Most trials in this book have had only one defendant. Such cases revolve entirely around the evidence against him or her alone and about what can be established about their character. Cases involving multiple defendants — 'multi-handers' as we call them in the profession — are very different. Even though a barrister will still represent only one of the individuals in the dock, having so many overlapping and sometimes contradictory pieces of evidence against multiple defendants makes these cases much more complicated. And one must employ different strategies.

One is to see if I can distinguish my client from their co-defendants. In a multi-hander what I really want to do is to get myself in a position whereby if the jury is going to convict anybody it's not going to be my client, and that if anybody is going to be acquitted the jury starts with my client. I applied this strategy in one of the best-known 'multi-hander' cases I fought — the phone hacking trial.

Held at the Old Bailey in London between October 2013 and May 2014, the trial was described by one commentator as the Trial of the Century. I'm not sure that sobriquet was quite deserved (although the century was quite young), but the case certainly attracted a lot of attention in the media. This may have been partly because several of its leading practitioners were among the accused.

Scotland Yard had been carrying out several investigations into newsgathering at Rupert Murdoch's newspapers, the *News of the World* and the *Sun*. Operation Weeting was into allegations that staff at the *News of the World* had intercepted or commissioned the interception of messages left on the mobile phones of public figures. Operation Elveden was a parallel inquiry into cash payments made by journalists on the *Sun* to public officials in exchange for information for stories.

The 'phone hacking trial' was the first and biggest in a series of prosecutions arising from these investigations. Two of the defendants were very well known: Rebekah Brooks, who had edited both newspapers, and her successor at the *News of the World*, Andy Coulson, who had become David Cameron's communications chief in Downing Street. Also on trial were Rebekah's husband

Charlie Brooks, the *News of the World*'s former managing editor, Stuart Kuttner, its former royal editor Clive Goodman — who had already served time in prison for phone hacking — and Mrs Brooks's personal assistant, Cheryl Carter.

My client was Mark Hanna, the former head of security at News International, Mr Murdoch's company. I was approached to represent Mr Hanna by a long standing solicitor friend, Ian Ryan, of Howard Kennedy, who had hired me to represent Colin Stagg in the Wimbledon Common case all those years ago.

Mr Murdoch's company was footing the legal bill for most of the defendants, meaning that money was no object. As a result, the case was remarkable for its gathering of high-powered legal talent. The defendants' barristers read like a *Who's Who?* of London QCs, with Mrs Brooks represented by Jonathan Laidlaw QC, Andy Coulson by Timothy Langdale QC, Cheryl Carter by Trevor Burke QC, and Stuart Kuttner by Jonathan Caplan QC. Clive Goodman, who was often too ill to attend, was represented by David Spens QC.

The prosecution had Andrew Edis QC and his junior, Mark Bryant-Heron QC.

With an exciting cast comprising famous individuals, a story of secrets, scandal and lies and with journalism itself on trial, the media followed the proceedings intently. Press seats in Court 12 were distributed by ballot. Those who failed to secure a seat in court could watch a live broadcast of the proceedings in an adjoining courtroom.

Reporters were especially interested in rumours suggesting that Rebekah Brooks and Andy Coulson had been having an affair while she edited the *News of the World*. Police had found an unposted letter from Mrs Brooks to Coulson in which she wrote of her affection for him. The prosecution successfully argued that extracts from the letter should be shown to the jury because it proved the pair were so intimate that they must have known what the other was doing when they worked together on the paper. I think its revelation was more embarrassing for him because he was married at the time of the relationship, but I'm not sure it helped the prosecution. Reading out passages elicited sympathy for the defendants, even though they had both been editors of tabloid newspapers.

Both Mrs Brooks and Coulson were dignified in court. I can only take people as you find them but she was very polite. When I had a bad cold she bought me some cough sweets. Coulson struck me as being more reserved than the other defendants. During the little contact I had with him he was courteous and I remember him coming up and thanking me for something I had said during my cross-examination of a witness, saying how much it had helped him. I felt he was somebody who couldn't quite believe that he had ended up in the dock at the Old Bailey. He was obviously a highly intelligent man who behaved with dignity, but he had probably fallen further than anyone.

Although the case centred on phone hacking and payments to public officials, Charlie and Rebekah Brooks and my client, Mark Hanna, were charged with conspiracy to pervert the course of justice. The prosecution alleged that they had disposed of potentially incriminating evidence about phone hacking or corrupt payments around the time she was arrested in July 2011.

Conspiring to pervert the course of justice is a serious offence, normally punishable by a prison term, and the evidence could have looked suspicious.

On Sunday 17 July, the Brookses had driven from Oxfordshire to London, with her going to Lewisham police station by appointment and him to their flat in Chelsea, leaving Hanna to drive the Brooks Range Rover from Oxfordshire to London. According to the police, Charlie Brooks then handed potentially damaging property to Mr Hanna for safekeeping. What was agreed by everyone was that some lesbian DVDs and a laptop belonging to Mr Brooks were later found by a cleaner stashed next to some bins in the underground car park of the flats where the Brookses lived. The police found nothing at all incriminating on the laptop, but the prosecution insinuated that other harmful material could have been dumped, even though there was no evidence of that.

Deploying my usual strategy in multi-handers, I sought to distinguish Mr Hanna from the others alongside him in the dock. His background, income, circumstances and status were completely different from his wealthy, professional co-defendants. Mrs Brooks had previously been

Britain's best known editor, while Coulson had worked for Number 10. Clive Goodman had been the royal editor and Stuart Kuttner the managing editor of the country's best-selling newspaper. These journalists had mixed with powerful people from politics, the royal family, business and entertainment. Charlie Brooks had been educated at Eton and was a racehorse trainer and racing diarist.

Unlike everybody else in the trial Mark Hanna was not a journalist of any kind. His job involved organising security at the company's London HQ and personal security when necessary for its directors and occasionally its reporters. When I analysed his rather grandiose title of Head of Security, he was often doing a rather mundane job, for example arranging the rotas of the company security guards. He had had a modest career in the British Army, during which he had served in Iraq and Northern Ireland. Right from the start I intended to highlight and exploit his Army record, modesty and sense of duty. He was a foot soldier on trial with the officers. He was also just doing his job. Nobody suggested he was paid a penny more for doing what he did, and in any event he had been following his instructions.

As well as portraying Mr Hanna as a minor player among more connected and powerful individuals, it was important to emphasise the insignificance of his alleged role in the great scheme of things. The victims of phone hacking included Princes William and Harry and two Home Secretaries and tens of thousands of pounds had been paid to a Ministry of Defence official and police officers. While serious in its own right, the charge of conspiracy to pervert the course of justice was something of a sideshow to these main attractions. Intending to emphasise the very minor role my client had in the supposed conspiracy, I sat right at the very back of the court throughout proceedings. I also deliberately steered clear of the daily and sometimes bitter skirmishes between the prosecution and the other defence lawyers.

Fortunately there was no need to put ourselves in conflict with the other defendants. In multi-handers, friction between those in the dock can spill over into public recriminations and conflicting accounts tend to damage the credibility of all concerned. The only people whose case impacted on Mr Hanna's were Charlie Brooks and to a lesser extent his wife. I was able to run our defence without attacking Mr Brooks because our case was not in conflict with his. His barrister, Neil Saunders, and I were contending that there never had been any agreement to hide incriminating material. Our defences were aligned.

The prosecution case was two-fold. Firstly, they contended that other unknown items of incriminating material must have been disposed of because the items that were found by the bins were so innocuous that the three accused wouldn't have gone to all that trouble to remove those alone. Secondly several of Mrs Brooks's iPhones and Blackberries had gone missing and nobody knew where they were. The prosecution had the beginnings of a case, but it was all based on assumption. Nevertheless, it still had the potential to tempt a jury.

There were also other complications. The prosecution relied upon some text messages between Mr Hanna and some of his security staff which appeared to be slightly incriminating. One read: 'The chicken is in the pot' which supposedly referred to the successful removal of damaging material. Some of Mr Hanna's hired security guards were due to face trial later for their parts in the alleged conspiracy. They were all ex-Army types who tended to use dramatic jargon. Other texts involved the collection of a pizza — which the prosecution implied was a suspicious piece of subterfuge and a code for something more incriminating, rather than ballast for Mr Brooks, who had been quaffing red wine while waiting for his wife to return from the police station. Much turned on the timing of when the pizza was ordered. Some poor soul from a High Street pizza chain had to give evidence as to what was ordered, when, and with what toppings. It was quite farcical.

I scored an early victory for my client long before the case for the defence began when, largely thanks to the hard work of my junior, Duncan Penny, I managed to scuttle the prosecution's telecommunications evidence. Duncan, who had run big prosecutions which relied on detailed analysis of mobile phone cell site evidence, realised that what the expert had extrapolated from his analysis of Mr Hanna's phone records couldn't be correct. The prosecution alleged that on the Sunday morning in question Mr

Hanna and a colleague had driven to the Brooks's home in Oxfordshire to collect the allegedly incriminating material, and adduced mobile phone evidence showing he was there for around 20 minutes, long enough to collect something.

But we had the mobile phone evidence examined by our own expert and his findings only confirmed what we suspected: when you analysed the phone mast evidence Mr Hanna had only actually been back at the house for a minute or two; nowhere near as long as the expert claimed. The mast that supposedly proved that they were there did not even provide a signal to that location. These were fundamental errors. I couldn't wait to cross examine the witness in court. But the element of surprise was crucial. Although we knew about it for months, my team didn't even discuss the phone evidence with the other defence lawyers in case someone from the prosecution overheard. I didn't want the Crown's barristers picking up on the error, doing some homework, and rectifying it — my tactical advantage would be lost.

Luckily the very busy prosecution lawyers didn't spot the mistake. The mobile phone expert appeared three months into the case — and it was pretty much my first serious intervention. The expert happily agreed to everything the Crown put to him during his evidence in-chief. It took me only an hour and a half to cross-examine him by which time he had shot himself in both feet and reloaded to repeat the exercise. By the time he returned to court after lunch he more or less admitted he had got one of the most important aspects of his evidence wrong.

After I had finished my cross-examination the judge tore him off a strip, telling him his evidence was a disgrace. I've never heard anything like it. The prosecution immediately said they would abandon his evidence and told the jury to forget everything the so-called expert had said. I didn't have any sympathy for the expert because he was giving evidence in an important case which could have resulted in my client going to prison. If you manage to destroy a piece of evidence it's in your interests to tell the jury that it was an extremely important piece of evidence and its destruction a serious blow for the prosecution.

I was yet to deal with the most important piece of evidence against my client, the discovery of the material in Chelsea, but nevertheless I had succeeded in destroying a plank of the case against him.

To reinforce the picture of him as a man set apart, I wanted Mark Hanna to give evidence so that I could delve into his background and character. I sought to portray him as someone who was completely out of his depth mixing in such exalted company. Almost all the other defendants had met Tony Blair. The only time my client had seen Tony Blair was on the television. Stuart Kuttner called the former Archbishop of Canterbury Robert Runcie as a character witness. I called Mr Hanna's next-door neighbour.

It was important for Mr Hanna to give his evidence

naturally. He freely acknowledged that he had taken Mr Brooks's laptop and some lesbian DVDs into lost property at News International at Wapping before they were returned to the car park below the Brooks's flat. But he denied there was anything incriminating. (Charlie Brooks later told the court that he had removed the pornography because he didn't want the police to leak it to the press.)

Had they been intending to ditch the laptop because it contained incriminating material then leaving it by the bins of the Brooks's flat didn't seem a particularly likely thing to do. In any case, Mr Hanna agreed that he had ample opportunity to dispose of any 'incriminating evidence' on the drive back from Oxfordshire to London. It didn't add up.

When the time came to deliver my closing speech, I moved from my position at the back of the court where I could only see the jury side-on and went up to the front row, a tactic I've deployed before. I said to the jury: 'I feel like I've just flown all the way from London to Sydney in tourist class and suddenly been upgraded to business class for the short hop to Melbourne.' I was pleased to see smiles on the jurors' faces, but I was not surprised. It's a line I've used before.

Turning to what I saw as the flimsy case against my client I gave a somewhat colourful characterisation of the Crown's case:

Here they are — Rebekah, Charlie and Mr Hanna. They

know Rebekah's likely to be arrested when she goes to the police station on Sunday evening. Charlie, who we're said to be conspiring with, is sitting in his house near Chipping Norton on Thursday. The prosecution say he's in possession of material that incriminates his wife, but he reads the Sporting Life, has a couple of gin and tonics, taps on the allegedly incriminating material and says to himself 'I'll leave that there until tomorrow'. Friday arrives, so he has a couple more gin and tonics, reads the Sporting Life again, looks at the incriminating material again, and decides to leave it where it is for another day. Now it's Saturday. Another read of the *Sporting Life*, a couple more gin and tonics, and lo and behold the incriminating material remains untouched. Is it likely that on Sunday he suddenly awakens and thinks 'Oh my God, what are we doing about the incriminating material? Phone Hanna! We've got to get rid of it'!

I was able to portray the whole scenario in a way that made it sound amusing and still made the point that if there was something incriminating it would have been dumped long before that Sunday morning. There was no reason to involve Mr Hanna in a last-minute panic. All the time I was on my feet I was looking at the jury and hoping to register a little smile or the odd chuckle. After I sat down the trial judge Mr Justice Saunders asked if I would accept the Oscar nomination for the most humorous speech in the case. I graciously accepted, but the purpose of the speech was not to amuse but to get across a serious argument in support of my client's case. The fact it could be done with humour made it easier to listen to, but did not diminish its message.

Shortly after the jury retired I had to start another case at Blackfriars Crown Court, where I was defending an indecent assault case against a German professor who had fathered 68 children by providing sperm donations to women he met online. I received a text message from my junior telling me Mr Hanna had been acquitted. By the time I had caught up with him after my court had risen, Mr Hanna and his solicitors had all rather stolen a march on me in the champagne stakes. So had many of the others. Andy Coulson, however, had been left in the dock — the only defendant to be found guilty.

I don't think the trial was politically-motivated. Undoubtedly some people tried to capitalise on Rebekah Brooks's and Andy Coulson's links to the Conservative Party, but I don't think that influenced the decision to prosecute. Because of the failure of earlier police inquiries to get to the bottom of the hacking, the investigation was pursued almost irrespective of cost, and I think the prosecution found themselves on a bit of a treadmill.

With the advantage of hindsight, I believe that the journalists could have been dealt with in a fairer, more effective way. Phone hacking appeared to be a widespread practice at the *News of the World* and apparently at other papers too, but I think that formal cautions could have been issued to the culprits along with a strong warning that anyone caught hacking in the future would be prosecuted. I think if that message had gone out loud and clear hacking would have been stopped in its tracks. The hacking victims could still have brought civil claims as indeed they did and there were some large payouts. Prosecuting the hackers was not really necessary.

Nonetheless, in the future only a genuinely rogue reporter, or a particularly stupid one, will attempt to hack anyone's phone, and they will deserve whatever punishment they get. If the trial achieved nothing else, that message will have been received.

AFTERWORD

A Life of Crime: Turning Over A New Leaf

~

Most people who come into contact with a barrister will encounter a clever, articulate and vigorously confident individual. Perish the thought, they may even appear arrogant. This is all a part of the act. An advocate who arrives at court looking timid, lacking in confidence and tongue-tied will never survive at the Bar.

As Head of Chambers I know there is massive insecurity among many, if not most barristers about the future of the profession and their place in it. They worry about where the next brief is coming from, how much work they will have next year, about how they will maintain their lifestyle, their standing, and their reputation. I think that has always been the case.

Being a barrister is a job without a guaranteed income or pension, or health insurance or sickness benefit or paid holidays. However illogical or daft, we feel we are only as good as our last case — and may never get another one.

Other professions have their stresses, too, of course. I don't think being a barrister is any more intense than being a GP. The headmaster of a big school will be under all sorts of pressure. What has changed is that barristers' income has declined relatively compared to other jobs. As a result of the cuts to Legal Aid, many barristers now earn significantly less than other professionals. In the 1950s and 60s and even 1970s, a barrister could afford to buy a townhouse in the better parts of London such as Chelsea or Putney. Nowadays they will be lucky to afford a one-bedroom flat on the outskirts of the capital.

Those who are very successful have nothing to complain about: they earn at least as much if not more than other professionals of their own age, such as GPs, headmasters or solicitors. Those doing plenty of Legal Aid work in the 1980s and 1990s when rates provided reasonable renumeration should have been able to make sensible financial provision for the future. But for the vast majority times are tough. Barristers who took out mortgages based on higher earnings a few years ago are faced with the prospect of downsizing to a smaller home.

Progress in other areas of life has had an impact on the life of the criminal barrister. The murder rate has plummeted because the ambulance service is reaching and treating people at the scene far quicker than they did 30 years ago and the treatment available at the scene is much better. A stabbing victim treated within five-to-eight minutes often survives when previously he would have died — and the crime becomes wounding with intent to cause grievous bodily harm rather than murder. Armed robbery is a crime that today's barristers rarely experience because bank security has improved with timelocks on tills and secret alarms.

Technology has also had an impact and though I can see its advantage of saving time, it saddens me that barristers are now more likely to visit crime scenes on Google Earth than on foot. Computers are able to search hundreds of thousands of documents to identify particular words thought likely to be significant in minutes rather than having lawyers go through each one individually.

Clients also use the internet to research barristers and increasingly instruct barristers direct, cutting solicitors out of the loop altogether.

Fortunately some things have stayed the same. By and large barristers still get on with each other and criminal cases are conducted reasonably without rancour. (A few people are notoriously difficult, but that's not necessarily because they are barristers, but it's because they are notoriously difficult people who have become barristers. You soon get to know who they are.)

We are still required to wear wigs. When you've worn one for as long as I have, it's like a second skin. I think it's ridiculous. The argument is that the wig gives you some sense of anonymity and I think some people think the youngsters like it because it makes them look a little older. Other people worry that abolition would ruin the second hand market and they'd never be able to sell the one they've got.

Some judges think the wig gives them an air of authority, but if you need a wig to exercise authority over your court you are not much of a judge. I think that justice is better done by the judge's words rather than by what he has on his head. The thought that you have to put part of a horse on your head to appear at a criminal trial is absurd. I don't mind a gown. Most jurisdictions require a gown, otherwise you don't know who's who. You need to be able to identify the lawyer.

At the age of 69, my fascination with the law and its working is undiminished. I still work every day from 6am to about 7pm. I am a bit less busy than I was, which is my choice, and I take more holidays.

Fifty years after I enrolled to study law at Bristol University, I can look back at my career with some perspective. I am glad I was called to the Bar; the cases have been endlessly and thrillingly varied. Some are almost impossible to lose; some nobody could win. But there is a group in the middle where the barrister can make a difference. So what I like doing more than anything else is reading a new case, because even after all these years I still feel that excitement. Is there something there that I can find that might win the case? How can I bring my experience and skills to bear? That moment when I am about to turn the first page still thrills.

ACKNOWLEDGEMENTS

When Martin Hickman from Canbury Press asked to come and see me in chambers I had no idea what he wanted. He had been a frequent visitor to the press benches in the trials involving the *News of the World* and the *Sun* newspapers of Rupert Murdoch's company News International. I assumed, wrongly, that it was another interview about one or other of the cases in which I had defended, the Head of Security of News International in the first and a journalist in the second.

When he asked me if I would accept a commission to write a book, I was frankly astonished. Why I thought, would anyone be interested in me or my career. We discussed it at length and he explained that if I were to agree he did not envisage a standard autobiography but rather a book aimed at non-lawyers trying to demystify the legal profession, explain how it works and including a synopsis of a few of the more interesting trials I had appeared in.

When I recovered from my surprise I gave some thought to the suggestion. He explained that it was unlikely to make me rich but would be an interesting challenge. I was also flattered; there are hundreds of barristers and he had selected me and I thought it might be nice for the family to perhaps have a record of my career. Anyway as is obvious from the fact that I am, writing this, I agreed and contracts were signed.

It soon became obvious to me that I had bitten off more than I could chew. Although used to writing legal opinions and submissions for court the act of writing a book is an altogether different skill set.

There was soon a further meeting with Martin and I explained that at the current rate of progress the book was going to take a decade or more to write, and work kept getting in the way. A solution was found in the jovial figure of John Troup. John, known as 'Troupy' to all, had been a fixture in Fleet Street since soon after leaving school and had become the East Anglia correspondent for the *Sun*. In the Metropolitan Police's campaign to stop journalists paying public officials for stories he was caught up in Operation Elveden and charged with paying £300 to a prison officer for information about the suicide of a prisoner. I had recently successfully defended the Head of Security of News International in the *News of the World* phone hacking trial and I was asked to defend Troupy. I agreed.

It is rare for a barrister to form a friendship with a client, particularly one charged with a criminal offence. It has only happened to me a couple of times in my career. However, Troupy was no ordinary client, in the first place I thought, and a jury subsequently agreed, that he was innocent. He was on trial with others and the case lasted for about 12 weeks. All the defendants were journalists or photographers working for the *Sun* and were entertaining company. Troupy is an educated, amusing, intelligent and sardonic man who was always ready with a quip or aside to relieve the courtroom tension or, more often, boredom. As the weeks passed we chatted and so a friendship developed. He had been made redundant by News International and had fallen on hard times, he was helping a friend in the butchery trade at the time of the trial.

So when it came to finding a solution for my inability to produce a manuscript I suggested that we needed a ghost writer and Troupy was the obvious candidate.

Without Martin and Troupy there would be no book. I owe to Martin the courage he had to commission me in the first place and I owe to Troupy thanks for all the hard work he put in when meeting me and recording our conversations and then converting them into the prose that we now have in the book. I owe each a huge debt.

There will of course be error and mistakes in the book. All are entirely my responsibility and I apologise for them in advance. There would have been more errors if friends who had worked with me on the cases had not taken the time and trouble to read and correct the proofs. I am grateful to all of them.

It is not possible to write about all that I have done in my career. Many of my clients expect and are entitled to have me treat our contact as confidential. I have not been able to write about my defence of David Duckenfield, who was the police officer in charge of the Hillsborough Stadium at the time of the tragedy when 96 Liverpool fans died and over 750 were injured; at the time of writing further litigation is pending and that chapter of the book has been removed to avoid any possible prejudice to ongoing cases. I also continue to sit as a part-time judge, and hence it would not be appropriate for me to comment on current judicial sentencing policy. All of that can wait for another day.

As the book has taken shape my dear wife, Gay, has read and re-read the drafts and corrected our spelling, grammar and syntax. As always I am grateful for all her help and support. My children and step-children have also read the drafts and provided both encouragement and corrections. Particular thanks to Robert who has taken time out from script writing in Santa Monica to make some incisive comments and suggestions. I am grateful to them all.

There would be no book and no career without the help of my parents who have supported me throughout and all those years ago bought me the wig and gown to start my career. I am still wearing the same wig!

Finally, I owe a huge debt to my clerks, firstly to John Grimmer who has been my senior clerk for 35 years. We have become friends and John has guided me throughout my career, assisted as he has been over the years by Paul, Trevor, Lee, Tom, Ellie, Gemma and Harry: just some of the clerks who have provided the essential support that all barristers need.

INDEX

INDEX

INDEX

Also by Canbury Press:

Beyond Contempt: The Inside Story
of the Phone Hacking Trial
by Peter Jukes
ISBN 978-0-9930407-7-1

www.canburypress.com